ON DIASPORA

On Diaspora

Christianity, Religion, and Secularity

D<small>ANIEL</small> C<small>OLUCCIELLO</small> B<small>ARBER</small>

CASCADE *Books* · Eugene, Oregon

ON DIASPORA
Christianity, Religion, and Secularity

Cascade Books
An Imprint of Wipf and Stock Publishers
199 W. 8th Ave., Suite 3
Eugene, OR 97401

www.wipfandstock.com

ISBN 13: 978-1-60899-400-7

Cataloging-in-Publication data:

Barber, Daniel Colucciello.

   On diaspora : Christianity, religion, and secularity / Daniel Colucciello Barber.

   xiv + 156 p. ; 23 cm. — Includes bibliographical references.

   ISBN 13: 978-1-60899-400-7

   1. Secularism. 2. Christianity and politics. 3. Cultural fusion. I. Title.

BL2747.8 B30 2011

Manufactured in the U.S.A.

Contents

Acknowledgments

THE EFFORTS TO WHICH we attach our own name are constituted by
many that we do not know, and by many others that we do not know
how to name. I am grateful, with regard to this particular effort, to know
how to name several individuals: Charlie Collier, for making this book
possible; Nathaniel Cunningham, for consistently vertiginous discussions
about what is at stake in this book; Brian Goldstone and Anthony Paul
Smith, for comments on drafts, conversations about the argument, and an
overarching intellectual friendship of the kind that pervades even one's in-
tuitions; and Erin Yerby, for things that bring me back to that point where
it becomes difficult to know how to name.

Introduction

THE IMPETUS BEHIND THIS book is not easily placed. It is concerned with matters that are proper to the theoretical practices that we call philosophy, theology, religious studies, anthropology, and cultural studies—which is to say that if this book is not easily placed, it is not because its concerns are simply foreign. The difficulty with placing this book derives instead from the fact that it is concerned with many matters. If it is peculiarly placed, then this is because of the constellation of its concerns. To say all of this, however, is not to provide an excuse for the nature of this book's concern (or constellation of concerns)—not at all. It is simply to distinguish, at the outset, the desire of this investigation. My contention—one, of course, that only the entirety of the text can bear out—is that there is a fundamental integrity to the book's approach, an integrity that simply could not be provided were one to accept the position of speaking from "within" any one (or two, or three . . .) of the theoretical practices I have mentioned. In other words, while I am concerned with matters proper to many theoretical practices, this is not because I find it important to create mixtures of theoretical practices for their own sake; it is rather because what matters for me is something that necessarily involves various theoretical practices.[1]

So what is it that matters for my investigation? It is, in the final instance, the concept of diaspora. It may seem odd to speak of diaspora as a concept and not as a sociological descriptor. There are, of course, very important advantages and insights to be gained from an empirically oriented account of diaspora, and my conceptually driven investigation should not

1. My insistence on addressing "what matters for thought" is indebted to Goodchild, *Capitalism and Religion*.

be understood as an implicit dismissal of these. That said, it seems to me that what is lacking from an empirical focus on diaspora is a consideration of the rather significant implications that diaspora may have for thought. It is one thing to characterize some phenomenon as being diasporic, but it is quite another thing to think of being itself as diasporic. This latter possibility is the one that intrigues me. The impetus for this book, then, is the intuition that diaspora, as a concept, as a noun-object of thought, bears a potential that is not fully articulated in its adjectival applications (where it is sufficient to say that a specific phenomenon is diasporic).

At the same time, it is by no means a simple matter to pose the question, What is diaspora?—and I should make clear that when I say it is not a simple matter, I mean not that it is difficult but that it is composite. Even if diaspora is to be conceived in itself, it cannot be approached in a direct manner, and this is because of the differential character of what the concept seeks to express. Diaspora, even as noun, opens onto a relation (or a relation of relations). To think about diaspora is to think about many things; diaspora matters, but it matters as an "intermattering" of many matters; it is named through the indirection of composition. This means that even an intentionally conceptual account of diaspora, with its desire to think what is presupposed by more empirical studies, finds itself involved in an irreducibly contingent endeavor of selection—that is, of selecting the matters through which the concept in itself is to be constructed. It is therefore the case that my account of diaspora, even as it is driven by a conceptual focus, will necessarily be a partial one. What, then, constitutes the partiality of this book? It is my selection of the concepts of Christianity, religion, and the secular. When I think about diaspora in what follows, I will think about it through these matters.

All three of these are concepts that claim to refer to empirical phenomena. Yet in addressing them I am primarily concerned with their conceptual character, with the way they function as theoretical operations that influence our patterns of thinking. My argument, with regard to each of these terms, is that they are intrinsically differential, that they are—each in its own way—characterized by an inconsistency.[2] It is, I will argue, only insofar as we fail to attend to this inconsistency, or only

2. A more developed and precise sense of how I use and intend this term will emerge in chapter 5. Yet I should say, at the outset, that inconsistency does not necessarily entail a negative or critical evaluation. Inconsistency, for me, points to a state of disequilibrium, of differential intensity, that has a valuable potential. What matters, then, is how one encounters and re-expresses this differential potential of inconsistency.

insofar as we treat it as an accidental feature, that we are able to maintain received understandings of what these concepts mean. Diaspora, then, is not just that which emerges as the differential relationship between Christianity, religion, and the secular; it is also—or more so—the differential relationship between the differential inconsistencies intrinsic to each of these concepts. The concept of diaspora is thus that which is engendered when the inconsistencies central to these three conceptual operations are foregrounded. Yet it is also a conceptual operation unto itself—one that is able, because it gives greater value to differential media than it does to origins and endings, creatively and compositively to conceive the inconsistencies of Christianity, religion, and the secular. The concept of diaspora is thus an intermattering effect constructed through the theoretical operation by which it addresses what it takes as its matters. If diaspora is a problem to be thought, I am trying to show, then it is this because of the problems that are presented by the concepts of Christianity, religion, and the secular.

The book, however, does not begin with a consideration of the differential constitution of any one of these terms. Chapter 1, "Immanence: Namelessness and the Production of Signification," addresses the theoretical paradigm according to which my investigation proceeds. This theoretical paradigm is one of immanence—or, keeping in mind the purposes for which it will be employed, one of diasporic immanence. Basically put, a paradigm of immanence is one in which the cause of being and the effects of being (i.e., all those particular beings or networks thereof) belong to the same plane. There is no transcendent point of reference, for each being is co-constitutive of every other being. I am especially interested in one consequence of immanence, which is that it becomes impossible to name being as such, even as the multitude of names given to beings (and to being in itself) point to the inescapability of signification. What I propose, then, is that immanence puts in play a reciprocal relay between namelessness and excessive signification. The chapter concludes by considering the way this paradigm of immanence informs the manner in which we approach the relation between philosophy and theology (or religion), as well as the way this paradigm's approach departs from the approaches set forth by rival (and in my view inadequate) paradigms.

It is then with chapter 2, "Diaspora," that the employment of this paradigm to the differential constitution of the already mentioned concepts begins. This chapter takes as its concern what I call "Christian declaration," understood as that which Jesus declares to be a real possibility of existence. I begin by attending to the fact that it is not difficult to counterpose what is declared, on one hand, to the course that the performance of historical Christianity has taken, on the other—this is the differential tension that resides in the concept of Christianity. The ease with which Christian declaration and Christian performance may be counterposed, I contend, is an effect of the failure to think Christianity according to the logic of diaspora. It is thus by foregrounding diaspora as a modality of understanding Christianity that one is able to evade counterposition of ideal and actual Christianities. This also, I argue, allows us to think Christianity in a more constructive manner, for if Christianity is diasporic then it can never exist in isolation from its others. I make this case by advancing diasporically inflected concepts of differential form, apocalyptic, and interparticularity.

Chapter 3, "The World in the Wake of Pauline Thought," continues the previous chapter's diasporic account of Christianity by interrogating the conceptual operations at work in Paul. I do not, however, address the entirety of the Pauline corpus, for my aim is to indicate, not just in the Christian declaration of Jesus but now in the key concepts of Paul, the theoretical knots in which the potentiality for a diasporic account of Christianity resides. Accordingly, the aim of this chapter is not to provide an evaluation of the full scope of Paul's thought, but rather to look at several indexes of differential tension. These indexes are the concepts of people, love, chaos, and world. They remain relevant not because they are concepts explicitly developed by Paul, but rather because they are concepts pulled out of his thought through the lens of diaspora. I argue that these concepts are indexes of "ambivalence" in Pauline thought and that this ambivalence—which is to say, the lack of an explicitly diasporic articulation of these concepts—is what enables much of what follows, in the wake of Paul, to emerge.

Chapter 4, "Christianity, Religion, and the Secular," makes the transition from the differential constitution of Christianity to the differential constitution of religion and the secular. The chapter seeks to unfold what follows in the wake of the ambivalences of Pauline thought. It tracks the invention of Christianity (beginning with Paul), and in doing so it argues that this invention required for itself another invention, namely that of religion. To speak of a concept's differential constitution is to refer to the inconsistency intrinsic to the concept. What this chapter does, then, is articulate the way in which the concept of Christianity, in order to resolve its inconsistency, mediated itself through the concept of religion, which came to bear the burden of this inconsistency. The chapter proceeds to track the later emergence of the concept of the secular, an emergence that also involves a transmutation of the concept of religion: Christianity established itself by establishing religion (such that it became the fulfillment of religion); the secular established itself by opposing itself to religion, and thus to Christianity as well (though in a problematically equivocal sense). I argue that the secular should be seen not as a successful resolution of these prior inconsistencies, but rather as yet another innovation in a series of inconsistencies.

Chapter 5, "The Differentiality of Differentialities," can be seen as a constructive complement to the criticism presented in chapter 4. If Christianity, religion, and the secular are marked (in their respective manners) by their intrinsically differential character, if they remain inconsistent, then what are we to do with them? What, in other words, is the way forward? The argument of chapter 5 is that the differentiality of each of these concepts must be seen not as something to be resolved—that, in fact, is precisely the strategy that these concepts have already implicitly followed. I call, then, for an alternative strategy, one in which the differentialities in question are to be affirmed. This is what it means to affirm the logic of diaspora: to see differentiality as an advantage, to think within the creative possibilities of difference as they emerge not only in each of the concepts in question, but also in the differential relations between the differentialities of these concepts. Accordingly, what this chapter offers is an account of ways in which these differentialities, as well as the differentiality of these differentialities, open new beginnings for thought.

Immanence

Namelessness and the Production of Signification

> Now the Lord said to DJ Spinoza,
> Get out of your country!
>
> And DJ Spinoza said to the Lord,
> What country are you talking about, Lord?
>
> —Eugene Ostashevsky[1]

The Paradigm of Immanence

IMMANENCE HAS ONTOLOGICAL IMPORT, but it begins as a manner of relation. An immanent relation is one in which neither term can be made utterly prior to the other; immanently related terms are mutually constitutive. This is the case even, or especially, when we consider relations of cause and effect. In this vein we might invoke Gilles Deleuze's commentary on Spinoza, where he remarks that in immanence the effect remains in the cause "no less than the cause remains in itself."[2] A certain asymmetry still obtains, for immanence accepts the possibility of distinguishing between cause and effect. The innovation thus lies not in a careless affirmation of

---

1. Ostashevsky, "Now the Lord Said to DJ Spinoza," 97.
2. Deleuze, *Expressionism in Philosophy*, 172.

simple indistinction, but more precisely in a refusal to convert the meaningful distinction of cause and effect into a relation of transcendence. In fact, it could be said that the meaningfulness of a distinction between cause and effect is preserved only by dint of an immanent relation. Relationality, after all, cannot be a one-way street, and so the cause, in order to meaningfully present itself as cause, must maintain a relation to its effects. If the cause is to be genuinely related to its effects, then it must be capable of being affected by what it effects. Immanence, then, is a two-way street, even as it maintains the possibility of distinguishing between cause and effect. The fact that effects remain in the cause just as much as the cause remains in itself means that the cause is affected by its effects. It is because of this affection that we say not only that effects are immanent to (or remain in) the cause, but also that the cause is immanent to (or affected by) its effects. The cause is not prior to its effects, for its essence is affected by what it effects; the cause is *constituted* by its effects. Immanence thus greatly impacts the way we conceive the relation between finite beings and an infinite being, where this latter being is understood in terms of a self-existing essence (which is classically named as God). The consequence, put simply, is that there is no longer any God beyond and unaffected by creatures, for the cause is produced by its effects.

It is here that we can see how the formal account of relations offered by immanence engenders a corresponding ontology: the being of the cause and the being of the effects belong to one plane of immanence. As Spinoza said, there is only one substance, composed of a multitude of modes. The distinction between a divine substance and created substances is thus precluded, at least insofar as it introduces two planes of being. These two planes, the transcendent and the dependent, cannot admit an immanent relation, and this is because the latter plane, as the effect of the transcendent cause, is not permitted to affect the constitution of the former plane. An immanence of relation can be preserved only alongside an immanence of being, or substance. Effects therefore are no longer separate substances from the cause; they instead become affections or modalities of the cause, singularities that determinately constitute—or *express*—the one and only substance.

How, then, should we conceive this one substance? It may be denominated, following Spinoza, as "God, *or* Nature."[3] I will say more below

3. Spinoza, *Ethics*, 114. For the sake of readability, I will hereafter render the phrase without italicizing "or."

on the complications involved in such a denomination, but it suffices presently to note the inadequacy of a reductive interpretation of Spinoza's act of naming. A reductive interpretation would be one in which Nature is taken as "really" meaning God or, more commonly, in which God is taken as "really" meaning Nature. This interpretive move falls short because it is unable to take seriously the non-objectivity of immanence; it fails to grasp the impossibility of resolving immanence into something that would be unaffected by the immanence of relation. Let us say, for now, that the term "Nature" functions to affirm immanence against the transcendent inclinations of theological thinking.[4] What is called God may just as well be called Nature, for Nature—understood as the open totality of being—is not conditioned by anything that would transcend it. At the same time, however, it would be a mistake to foreclose theological denomination, given the condition that such naming of God is delinked from the invocation of the transcendent. It is, in fact, quite possible to understand Spinoza's denomination of "God, or Nature" as a radicalization—or fulfillment—of the Jewish desire to understand that God is One.

4. When I refer here to "theological thinking," or when I refer later to theological discourse, a confusion might emerge regarding the nature of my interaction with a properly theological enterprise. It could be said that commitment to an approach that focuses on religion—that foregrounds religion rather than theology—has among its advantages a certain pluralism (for does not theology tend to turn back on Christian claims as normative?) as well as a sense that what matters are not just theoretical claims about God but also, or even moreso, practices or embodied habits. I should say right away, and as directly as possible, that I find it essential to affirm both of these advantages, and thus I would not want my selection of the term "theological" to be understood as an implicit rejection of them (or of the ability of the discourse of religion to advance them in ways that the theological cannot). So why, if this is the case, do I refer to theological thinking and discourse, rather than to religious thinking and discourse? It is, quite simply, because I am working within a Spinozian context in which the question of God is at stake, and so—*strictly speaking*—it is a question of *theos*. My concern, at least initially, is how the concept (or even name) of God enters into relation with, or is produced out of, a theoretical practice. It is therefore because this book begins as an investigation into the theoretical practices that engender or are implicated in the concept and signification of God that I refer primarily to the theological rather than to the religious. (Though later in the book there will be a more explicit discussion of the concept of religion.) In other words, what directs my reference to the theological is not a desire to make the theological into something that would be normatively prior to the connotations and scope of the religious; it is rather the specificity of the contingently theoretical tasks to which I have just adverted. Indeed, though reasons of theoretical specificity will lead me to refer initially to the theological (rather than to the religious), my broader commitment to the above-mentioned advantages possessed by a focus on religion (rather than on theology) is indicated by my use, later in this chapter, of religious discourse as a synonym of theological discourse.

As Steven Smith claims, Spinoza's *Ethics* "takes to heart and with the utmost seriousness the Shemah, the biblical injunction known to every Jew: 'Hear O Israel, the Lord is God, the Lord is One.'"[5] The interpretation that understands God as a kind of code for Nature not only skirts over the question of signification (for if God is "really" meant to signify Nature, what does it mean that God is nonetheless invoked as sign?), it also remains—at least implicitly, or even unconsciously—within the very paradigm Spinoza seeks to dissolve. This is to say that a simple opposition between Nature and God, where the latter is reduced to the former, continues to operate within the non-immanent polarity of transcendence. Of course, the direction is reversed—Nature is no longer dependent on God, rather God becomes dependent on Nature—but the denial of immanence is maintained. In short, what a reductive interpretation loses is the oscillating identification—or to borrow an Adornian term, the nonidentity—of God and Nature that enables Spinoza to install an immanent relation between two poles normally separated.

The conversion from a formal insistence on immanent relationality to ontology is brought about through an account of expression. Being is expressive; it is nothing more and nothing less than the expression of God. The key to avoiding a transcendent account of expression is to set forth the simultaneity of expression and construction.[6] Substance is expressive, such that its expression is auto-constructive. To say that effects expressively construct the cause is to say not that God is something already existing that is *consequently* expressed (whether imitatively, analogically, or dialectically), but rather that God *is* expression. As Deleuze, again commenting on Spinoza, puts it: there is a "double immanence of expression in what expresses itself, and of what is expressed in its expression."[7] The immanent relation of cause and effect, or of God and creatures, has its being in expression, which is to say in the construction of what is expressed. There is, it will be observed, a certain circularity here: that which is expressed can be found only in expression, yet expression constructs what is expressed.[8] This paradox is only amplified when we recall that immanence

5. Smith, *Spinoza's Book of Life*, 18.

6. Éric Alliez asserts that immanence, as it emerges through the figures of Spinoza and Deleuze and Guattari, must be understood in virtue of "the great identity EXPRESSIONISM = CONSTRUCTIVISM." See Alliez, *Signature of the World*, 103.

7. Deleuze, *Expressionism in Philosophy*, 180.

8. As John Mullarkey has observed, one demand that emerges in view of Deleuze's

cannot be related to something unaffected by the immanent relation, for this would be to make immanence immanent *to* something—it would be to deny immanence. Indeed, Deleuze, writing with Félix Guattari, claims that "immanence is immanent only to itself"—that is, immanence is immanent neither to nothing nor to something.[9]

Immanence, then, is irreducible and autonomous. It cannot be reduced to something, for to do so would be to deny the immanence of that something to all other things. Concomitantly, we can say that immanence is autonomous, for the laws of its expression are given by nothing other than this very expression. Yet this returns us to the paradox mentioned above, that of properly naming immanence. It is fine to assert that all things are immanently related, such that all things immanently— and thus equally, or univocally—express being. The difficulty arises when we attempt to name this being (or in Spinoza's terms, this substance). To say that "immanence is immanent only to itself," or to add perhaps that immanence is autonomous, is to affirm, through a methodological or formal principle, that all things are immanently related. But what, then, *is* immanence? On one hand, we can answer this question through expression: immanence is whatever is expressed. This is the diachronic aspect of naming immanence, for it affirms all things as equally expressing immanence, and insists that whatever emerges is also and equally expressive of immanence. On the other hand, there is the synchronic aspect of naming immanence, and it is this aspect that presents a greater difficulty. While it is obviously possible to pursue an additive approach to immanence, which would involve enumerating all things (and more importantly the relations of all things), this approach is still not sufficient, for the question returns: all of this expresses immanence, but what is the immanence that is expressed?

Spinoza, I have already noted, called it "substance."[10] But he also called it "God, or Nature." In what follows, I would like to argue that this additional act of naming stems from a logic of necessity. It is not, in other words, merely contingent or strategic—though we could claim that it follows a

philosophy of immanence is "to reconcile [his] normative philosophy of creation with a descriptive naturalism" (*Post-Continental Philosophy*, 44).

9. Deleuze and Guattari, *What is Philosophy?*, 45. Further on in the passage they claim that "whenever immanence is interpreted as immanent *to* Something, we can be sure that this Something reintroduces the transcendent."

10. For instance, Spinoza remarks: "God is unique, that is, that in Nature there is only one substance, and that it is absolutely infinite" (*Ethics*, 10).

strategic *necessity*. This is to say that even as the names of God and Nature are contingent, occupying a specific function in the history of discourse inherited by Spinoza, the act of naming is not contingent. Even though the specific names that are put in play may be traced to the contingencies of a particular conjuncture, the act of naming itself remains necessary.

Why is it necessary to undertake an act of naming? We can begin by recalling the difficulty engendered by the requisite refusal to make immanence immanent to something. This leaves us with an immanence that is autonomous, an immanence that is, as it were, in itself. Yet immanence, if we think of it as simply in itself, suddenly becomes something transcendent. Immanence cannot just be in itself, for this would make immanent relation into an object, into something that precedes the enactment or deployment of immanent relation. In short, immanence in itself becomes the transcendent point of reference for all immanent relations—and this is, of course, to contravene immanence. What must therefore be grasped is that immanence, properly speaking, is nameless. The fact that we contravene immanence in the very act of naming it, even when we strip it of all names—of every something—except immanence in itself, makes manifest the irreducibility of immanence to a name. The irreducibility of immanence exerts its force even on the autonomy of immanence. It is along these lines that I take the import of Rocco Gangle's remark that "Immanence does not realize one possible figure of thought. It is not a framework, template or schema. It does not interpret. It unlocks."[11] The notable danger is thus that immanence, in the very act of refusing its immanence to something (to a figure of thought) by means of the assertion of its autonomous existence as immanence in itself, becomes its own figure of thought.

Immanence is therefore irreducible to a name, even the name of immanence (or substance). Nonetheless, we cannot avoid naming it. To say that immanence is expressed in its effects begs the question of the cause that is in immanence with, and is constructed by, its effects. Furthermore, we must observe that, diachronically speaking, expression is never final, for there is always the emergence of new expression (or the dynamic of re-expression). The question again arises: What is it that, even as it is expressed, enables the emergence of new expression, or the act of re-expression?

11. Gangle, "Theology of the Chimera," 42. The volume in which this essays appears, *After the Postmodern and the Postsecular*, stands at the vanguard in contemporary attempts to think in novel ways about the relationship between continental philosophy and questions of religion.

Immanence, though it is properly nameless, must be named. Every name given to immanence must be improper, for immanence is properly nameless, yet it is proper to name immanence. There is, in short, an improper propriety involved in the act of naming immanence. The consequent task is thus to name immanence, to give it an improper name, while simultaneously affirming its proper namelessness. I contend that it is precisely this task that Spinoza fulfills when, having claimed that the immanence of cause and effects means there is nothing but substance, he remarks that this substance may be called—i.e., named—"God, or Nature."

If we say that immanence is substance, and say nothing more, then we fall prey to the assumption that immanence, which is nameless, has been properly named. Substance, of course, has the connotation of neutrality, of being a name that adds nothing to what it names (in this sense it resembles the naming of immanence as immanent only to itself). But to rest in this connotation would be a mistake, for it would be to conceal that there *is* an act of naming. It is precisely this concealment that is precluded when Spinoza adds to the name of substance the additional names of God and Nature. There is a doubling, in two senses: first, the purportedly proper naming of immanence as substance is doubled by the naming of "God, or Nature"; second, this double of substance is itself doubled into God and Nature. Spinoza can be understood as making explicit, through this doubling, the necessity of signification—the necessity, that is, of naming that which is nameless.[12] There is an excessiveness, an impropriety, in naming

12. It should be noted that, for Deleuze's account of Spinoza, expression and signification are mutually exclusive, such that the latter is to be rejected in favor of the former. For Spinoza, he says, "two domains" are severed from one another: "that of expression and of the expressive knowledge which is alone adequate; and that of signs, and of knowledge by signs, through apophasis or analogy" (*Expressionism in Philosophy*, 180). Though my use of "signification" throughout this book may fairly be understood as a departure from Deleuze, I should first make clear my initial agreement with this distinction that he observes. Expressive knowledge concerns an immanent encounter with the real, whereas signification falsely supposes that the real may be apprehended through possession of the proper sign. Yet there is no proper sign—as I am presently arguing, immanence is properly nameless, its expression exceeds all proprietary naming ("possession of the proper sign"), and so signification is fictive from beginning to end. The "knowledge" involved in signification, Deleuze notes, "remains of the first kind" (181), which is to say that it belongs to the imagination rather than to the real. My position is thoroughly in agreement with all of this. Nonetheless, I proceed by speaking of signification because of my desire to take seriously—to think through in a structural manner—the inevitability of signs. My aim is to valorize signification not as that which possesses the truth of the real, but rather as the necessary excess of the immanently nameless real. Such an aim

the immanence that is nameless, and the only way of thinking this excess is to perform it. Note however that the operation I am here tracing is not identifiable with the logic of negative theology. While it is the case that negative theology also grapples with the difficulty of naming the nameless, it is equally the case that negative theology addresses this difficulty by signifying that the object of signification is unsignifiable. Immanence, however, cannot permit this strategy, for such a strategy makes the unsignifiable into something that transcends signification. What is required, on the contrary, is an immanence of the nameless with every name that is given to the nameless. It is for this reason that the Spinozian approach to the difficulty of signification is one of doubling: the nameless is necessarily doubled by names that are—by the same necessity—improper, but these names must simultaneously enter into an immanent relation with namelessness. This is to say, then, that the signification put into play by the act of naming is fictive not because it falls short of the nameless, but because it emerges from the constitutive excess of the nameless. Signification is fictive because it cannot correspond to an immanence that is properly nameless, but the fiction thus set forth is nonetheless real. The fiction belongs to immanence not because it properly names immanence (it does not—that is why it is fictive), but because its impropriety and contingency is produced by the propriety and necessity of naming immanence.

What this means is that there is an ineffaceable—yet essentially productive or excessive—relay that takes place between immanence in itself, which is nameless, and the fictive but necessarily generated contingent names given to immanence. This movement of the real is indicated by Spinoza's own acting of naming, which refuses to provide a single proper name and instead sets forth a relay between substance (the purportedly proper name) and God/Nature (names that excessively signify). The ineffaceability of this relay is indicated, furthermore, by the relay set forth, *within* signification, between God and Nature. There is, first, a relay between namelessness (substance) and signification (fictive names of God and Nature), but in order for this relay to be maintained in its immanence, there must be a second relay, and this last occurs between the fictive names. The second relay is required because these fictive names,

---

should be seen as a supplementation—not a contravention—of Deleuze's interpretation: it is not to deny the primacy of expression to signification, it is rather to observe and to conceive the excessive, improper, and inevitable material of signification that is produced by this very primacy.

even as they signify the nameless, must signify both the namelessness of what they signify (Nature) and the necessity of excessively signifying the nameless (God).

We could say that the relay between namelessness and signification is relayed by the relay, within signification, between God and Nature. This is, admittedly, a somewhat cumbersome formulation, but it serves to highlight the sort of relays that are necessary if we are to signify immanence in such a way that immanence is not thereby contravened. Only in this way do we avoid the twin dangers that haunt immanence: that of letting namelessness transcend names and that of making names transcendent to the nameless. The two names of Spinoza's equivocation—God and Nature—signify distinct yet egalitarian tendencies of immanence. God names what might be understood as a maximalizing or amplificatory tendency, one that takes the necessity of signifying immanence to the highest power. From this vantage, being is not mere being, it is instead something that must be said, something that, as it is signified, calls upon and is invested with a plenitude of meaning and desire, such that being is envisioned as always more, always other. As Gangle observes: "God, as Spinoza himself saw, is *the* singular term drawn from the Western tradition of thinking, the radical self-contradictoriness and inconsistency of whose 'saying' lends it unique capacities to express immanence in the most powerful way."[13] Nature, on the other hand, names a minimalizing or deflationary tendency, one that legitimately poses the critical question: is being, in fact, rightly signified when we say so much about it? From this latter vantage, the constructions that carry such meaning and desire begin to appear as improper fictions, significations foisted onto intrinsically mute being. The inconsistency of such significations becomes a condition for the divestment of belief and the affirmation of the proper namelessness of immanence.

Immanence, as I am articulating it, refuses to choose between these tendencies. It insists instead on the validity of both and sees in each the relay of the other. This is no dialectic, at least not where dialectic involves the passing from one side to another, again and again, in order to come closer to a reality that passes beyond each side.[14] Against

13. Gangle, "Theology of the Chimera," 41.

14. It should not be presumed that Hegel's thought is identifiable with this sort of characterization of the dialectic. The ultimate account of why this identification cannot be made is provided by Crockett, Davis, and Žižek, *Hegel and the Infinite*.

this, what immanence demands is reciprocal constitution, a duality that may be understood perhaps as more than unity, or perhaps as less than unity, but in every case can never be fixed in relation to unity (which is irreducibly doubled as "God, or Nature"). The necessity of immanence's namelessness and the necessity of signifying immanence are reciprocal; the only unity lies in the reciprocal necessity of this relay. What matters, then, is not to make these two tendencies determine one another such that they achieve a mutual synthesis or nihilation. The key is to enable this relay—which includes disenabling situations in which one tendency becomes transcendent to the other—and in doing so to intensify the capacity to constructively express immanence.

It is along these lines that it becomes possible to speak of immanence in terms of surplus. This is not, of course, to posit a transcendent something called "surplus."[15] More precisely, what surplus names is the dynamical relation between the two sides of immanence, God and Nature. In this relation, God and Nature, or signification and namelessness, imply one another yet retain an exteriority to one another. Surplus thus concerns the mutual displacement that proceeds from immanent relation. On one hand, signification is a surplus exceeding namelessness, for its fictive production of names articulates a power of immanence to exceed the muteness of mere givenness; on the other, namelessness is a surplus exceeding the relations of logical possibility and limitation that are engendered by signification. It is precisely because of this exteriority of each to the other that the dynamical relation of immanence can get rerouted through—which is to say congealed in—the transcendent. For instance, signification, when it turns the world into something that bears a privative relation to God, forgets that the God it names is immanent to Nature. From the other side, naturalism, when it begins to imagine immanence as something already given yet obscured by signification, commits the error of conceiving immanence as something that transcends all names. What becomes evident from these exemplary errors is that the exteriority of one side, if it is to avoid emplotting a transcendent point of orientation, requires the displacement of the other side. There is surplus only on the condition that this surplus avoids the respective reifications (which involve making immanence immanent to something) of God and Nature. Surplus, then, is *nothing* other than the immanence of relation

15. Though my use of this term differs from her own use, my adoption of it is indebted to Kordela, *$urplus*.

between the exteriority of signification to namelessness and the exteriority of namelessness to signification.

Rival Paradigms

I have thus far sketched the theoretical paradigm of "immanence" that will be at work throughout this text. The aim of giving explicit attention to this paradigm is to help clarify the interests and conceptual operations motivating the arguments that follow. As a means, then, of giving a greater degree of determinacy to this paradigm, and of making clear the ways in which this paradigm can intervene within and push beyond the present possibilities of thought regarding the relation of Nature and God, here transposed as the relation of philosophy and theology, I will now turn to a critical examination of rival paradigms of this relation.

A couple of initial clarifications may be beneficial. First, the aim here is not to give an exhaustive catalog of the ways in which theological discourse is philosophically positioned. It is rather to look at those tendencies that either have a strong influence—which is to say that they command a notable degree of attention—or provide an innovative mode of approach (some tendencies, of course, may meet both of these criteria). There will be those who claim that one paradigm or another has been left unexamined, and such a claim may very well turn out to be true. Nonetheless, my goal is not to furnish an encyclopedic account, but rather to assay the elements that compose the set of immanence's most interesting rivals. Second, my aim is not to make available comprehensive accounts of these tendencies. The concern lies, more precisely, with the various manners in which these paradigms converge and diverge with immanence. Thus there will be those who find my accounts of these paradigms to be partial, stylized, and even polemical. Such impressions, however, are unavoidable given the approach I am adopting, which is centered on my own paradigm of immanence and on the ways in which it evaluates the field of alternative paradigms.

The first of these paradigms can be termed "Philosophical Delimitation" (PD). The distinguishing characteristic of this paradigm is its insistence on the primacy of a purely philosophical structure, along with the concomitant evaluation of theological discourse from the vantage of such a structure. For this paradigm, the valorization or devalorization of theological discourse is derived from the prior condition of a philosophical structure. One notable exemplar of this paradigm may be found in Immanuel Kant, who, having first set out the nature and scope of reason, proceeded to delineate the precise domain in which religious conceptuality could function legitimately—hence the need for an account of religion within the boundaries of mere reason. What is important here is not the specific value (or lack thereof) granted to theological discourse, but rather the manner in which this evaluation becomes possible. Kant, for instance, was able to affirm certain aspects of religion while denying others, but his essential move resides not in this specific admixture of affirmation and denial—it lies, more basically, in the way that a purely philosophical approach sets the conditions for all affirmations and denials.

Kant's approach, as I have adumbrated it, is by no means singular, for it can be located in various figures. The one to which I prefer to give some attention is Martin Heidegger, and this is because it is with him that the ontological stakes of this paradigm become most explicit. In an early essay, "Phenomenology and Theology," Heidegger asserts that theological discourse has a place, but that this place is given by an intrinsically philosophical (which at this moment in Heidegger's thought means phenomenological) orientation. Philosophy, by right, articulates the ontological horizon that sets forth the condition of possibility for the inescapably ontic discourse of theology.[16] Later in his philosophical progression, Heidegger will make a separate claim that nonetheless repeats the paradigm of philosophical delimitation. This later claim stems from his concern to think being in itself, apart from its manifestation in beings or its delimitation by ontotheological discourse. Statements about God, Heidegger observes, must be classified together with all other statements regarding beings.[17] This is because God, as a being, depends—like all other beings—on a pre-entitative ontological horizon, i.e., on the horizon of being itself. Thus, while the early Heidegger grants theological discourse a circumscribed degree of legitimacy insofar as it addresses the event of Christ, the later

16. Heidegger, commenting on the relationship between the concepts of "sin" (theological) and "guilt" (ontological), remarks: "if sin . . . is to be interpreted in theological concepts, then the *content* of the concept *itself*, and not just any philosophical preference of the theologian, calls for a return to the concept of guilt. But guilt is an original ontological determination of the existence of Dasein." See "Phenomenology and Theology," 51.

17. Heidegger, *Introduction to Metaphysics*. "We say, 'God is.' 'The earth is.' 'The lecture is in the auditorium.' 'This man is from Swabia'" (93). Heidegger proceeds to give many additional examples, but the point is clear, and he makes it explicit later on the text: "it is the same simple 'is'" (94).

Heidegger opposes it at the root insofar as it seeks to address the being of God. The God expressed by theological discourse never refers to anything greater than a being—a being, moreover, whose conditions of thinkability depend on the prior, purely philosophical endeavor to think being in itself. Accordingly, the opposition between philosophy and theology cannot be compromised. Any mitigation of this opposition would permit theology to confuse its discourse about a being with the conditions of possibility for such discourse and in this way to transgress its limits.

Viewed from a certain angle, this paradigm appears to be coterminous with the immanence I am advancing. There is, in other words, a kind of agreement insofar as I am refusing to think theological discourse within its own terms, i.e., self-referentially. Immanence, like Kant or Heidegger, seeks to position theological discourse within a wider vantage, a vantage that can, furthermore, qualify as philosophical. There is, nonetheless, a significant parting of ways between the paradigm of PD and that of immanence. This departure can be seen if we keep in mind that, for PD, theological discourse is understood as a specific borrowing or deployment of a more fundamental and generic mode of thought that is properly philosophical. Philosophy here functions as the universal horizon that places the particular theological discourse. For immanence, however, the schematization of philosophy and theology along the lines of the universal and the particular does not hold. This would only be the case if it were admitted that Nature properly names immanence, such that philosophy, in its immediate apprehension of substance, sets the conditions for theological discourse's production of names. Yet this is precisely what I have denied by asserting the reciprocal dynamic between namelessness and signification, i.e., the two equally necessary sides of immanence. It becomes important here to recall one of the dangers involved in thinking immanence: letting namelessness become transcendent to signification, to the fictive names that help articulate the surplus of immanence. PD falls prey to this danger when it treats the signifying operation of theological discourse as something that must be evaluated from a point of view that holds superior veracity (a point of view that I have exemplified as Kantian or Heideggerean philosophy).

PD is thus marked by a noticeable self-forgetfulness, or dearth of self-awareness, with regard to the matter of signification. It proceeds as if signification, with its excessive, improper naming, is something that belongs solely to theological discourse. What is obscured is that the proper names of Kant's "reason" and Heidegger's "being" are in fact not at all proper, that they too are engendered by the signifying operation of the substance to which they claim to immediately correspond. A specific consequence of PD's failure is evident in Heidegger's presumption that God must be understood as *a* being, rather than as being itself. It may, of course, be somewhat harsh to call this a presumption, given the coherence of Heidegger's claim—after all, if being is what God has in common with non-divine beings, then God must be classified on their side rather than on the side of being as such. At the same time, Heidegger's conclusion is severely counterintuitive insofar as the name God seems to intend something that encompasses the entirety of reality. Immanence provides a way of cutting short this counterintuitive line of thought by allying God with signification, such that God becomes an improper name, contingently engendered by the necessity of signifying immanence, for immanence in its namelessness—for what Heidegger would call being. Heidegger, then, is right to assert that God is not the same as being, but he is wrong to conclude that God must therefore be a being, for in doing so he leaves out the possibility of God functioning as a signification of being. The reciprocal constitution of immanence might thus be rewritten, with and beyond Heidegger, as "God, or Being."

The second paradigm is that of "Theological Particularism" (TP), which maintains an inverse relation to the paradigm of PD. This is because, for TP, what is central is to assert the primacy of theological discourse in its particularity. Whereas PD would argue for a fundamentally philosophical horizon that sets the conditions for the placement of particular discourses (theological discourse being one such particular discourse), TP is marked by the refusal of precisely such a placement. One could say that, in TP, theological discourse places itself, for the validity and content of theological discourse are no longer conceived in reference to a prior horizon. Instead, theological discourse constitutes its own horizon, it operates in an auto-referential manner. There are, of course, various versions of this auto-referential articulation, but the most noted exemplar is Karl Barth, for whom the primary locus of particularity is the Word as expressed in Jesus Christ, such that theology in its particularity provides the horizon for thinking the world.

TP's refusal of any transcendental or regulative horizon is motivated by two basic concerns. First, and perhaps prominently, there is the concern to preserve the seriousness and immediacy of theological discourse.

These are lacking when theological discourse is seen merely as the coded (and often partial and diluted) manifestation of a latent, universally apprehensible content. The second concern is that, philosophically speaking, it is not possible to set forth a universal discourse that would condition every particular discourse. In this regard, TP allies itself with philosophers such as Alasdair MacIntyre and Ludwig Wittgenstein,[18] who assert the irreducibility of particular discourses—as traditions and language-games, respectively—to any universal horizon. Theological discourse, conceived as such a tradition or language-game, is thus granted a specific autonomy that does not need to pass through more generic conditions of possibility or thinkability.

Immanence is in agreement with TP's critique of a transcendental, universalizing philosophical horizon. Like TP, immanence opposes the tendency, characteristic in PD, to blunt the signifying power expressed in theological discourse—there can be no setting of limits or of legitimating criteria, for the proper namelessness of immanence does not provide a form of *judgment over* signification, rather it provides a *relay of* signification. It is in view of this last point, however, that a question more critical of TP emerges. Does TP, in defending the power of signification expressed by theological discourse against PD's transcendental strictures, also provide signification with an immanent relation to namelessness? Or, to put the criticism more directly: Does not TP fall prey to a danger inversely related to the one to which PD succumbs? It seems so—that is, whereas PD made namelessness into something that transcends signification, TP, seeking to defend such signification, makes it into something that transcends namelessness. This is to say that TP forgets that immanence is properly nameless, that every name of immanence—including God—will be improper. Thus, while TP rightly asserts the capacity to signify immanence in a particular and non-diluted manner, it confuses this proper capacity to produce improper names, this necessary production of contingent names, with the proper signification of immanence.

What is to be opposed, then, is TP's auto-referentiality. It is not false to claim that the meaning of a statement made by a particular network of signification must involve recourse to the language-game or tradition of such a particularity. Difficulty arises, however, with the forgetfulness that this signification is fictive, or that it is a contingent production that

18. See, for instance, Brad Kallenberg's *Ethics as Grammar*.

draws on the surplus character of immanence. A particular theological discourse is not conditioned by PD's transcendental horizon, but it is conditioned by the ontological production—the mutually constituting relay between namelessness and signification—of immanence. TP's fundamental weakness lies in its disavowal of the latter point. This is evident in the fact that even as Karl Barth commendably demonstrated the ways in which theological discourse departed—whether antagonistically or dialectically—from the conceptual arrangements of regnant philosophies (and even of traditional theologies), he continued to assert, quite straightforwardly, that the truth of theological discourse resides in the Word of God. There is no questioning of signification itself, for all signification is grounded in the Word-object that it signifies. The impressive array of critical insights enabled by this strategy captures attention, but what most deserves attention—and criticism—is the unquestioned and comparatively monotonous auto-referentiality that subtends these insights. It can be said, then, that the discourse of TP is essentially contingent and improper, but that its auto-referentiality obscures this when it identifies God as the first and last name. Alongside any name, even the name of God, there is namelessness, and the limit of TP resides in its inability to affirm that its entire endeavor takes place within and because of—as an immanent relay of—this namelessness.

The third paradigm may be termed "Theological Ontology" (TO), and this is because of its claim that the desire to think being, or any universal horizon, is to be affirmed, but that this desire may only be fulfilled through theological discourse. TO shares TP's valorization of an auto-referential theological discourse and its concomitant opposition to the restrictions inherent in PD. At the same time, TO is far more willing than TP is to embrace a universal or ontological horizon. The line between TO and TP is, admittedly, a fine one, but there are abiding differences, if only at the level of emphasis. This is to say that whereas TP tends to valorize theological discourse by calling into question the very viability of foregrounding an ontological horizon and by emphasizing the distinctiveness of theological discourse, TO tends to valorize theological discourse by commencing with the universal aim of an ontological horizon and by arguing that this horizon is best apprehended by means of theology. Accordingly, while both TP and TO might agree that it is only (or at least preeminently) with theology that one finds the proper means of thinking being, their respective means of reaching this conclusion differ significantly.

This paradigm is, classically speaking, the most popular—one finds it throughout the patristic period, where it is consistently argued that Christianity is the true philosophy. For my purposes, however, the most notable instance of TO is found in the thought of Thomas Aquinas. This instance is noteworthy because of its explicit attempt, by means of analogy, to synthesize the theological and the ontological. It is as if one sees simultaneously the convergence and divergence between theological and ontological inquiries. This analogical approach has received significant contemporary attention, most innovatively in the work of John Milbank. The noted enemy of this innovative Thomism is Duns Scotus. Such animosity is to be expected, for it was Scotus who first insisted on the univocity of being—that is, on the necessity of thinking being in itself, prior to (or at least within and through) its distribution in beings. Scotus's prioritization of a properly ontological horizon is thus the ancestor of PD. Against Scotus—which is also to say against Heidegger—TO contends that theological discourse and ontological discourse, God and being, are convertible. It therefore becomes imperative not to think being as something that conditions the emergence of all beings (including God), but instead to think being as the analogy between, on one hand, an eminent God, and on the other, all beings, which are given by (and analogically participate in) being in its eminence (God).

From the vantage of immanence, TO can be seen as a useful corrective to TP's refusal to address in any positive manner the relationship between theological discourse and discourse on being. As I mentioned above, the auto-referentiality of TP can easily become a monologue that lacks any link to a larger horizon—one is left simply to expand and elaborate the expression of God. TO can thus be understood as an attempt to articulate the way in which any expression of God is likewise an expression of being. There is certainly value in this endeavor, for signification (to which theological discourse belongs) and being cannot be separated. At the same time, the advance made by TO in this respect involves a corresponding weakness, one that concerns the question of the relation between theological discourse and alternative discourses. TP fails to link signification to a more expansive horizon of being, for it rejects from the beginning the very possibility of such a horizon—yet this failure, or rejection, also allows it to give place to alternative discourses. The lack of any universal horizon implies not only that the signification of theological discourse cannot be evaluated from the outside, but also that alternative manners of signification cannot be evaluated from the outside (nor can they be evaluated by theological discourse). This means that TP maintains the logical possibility of a pluralist orientation. TO, however, abandons this possibility when it advocates the convertibility between God and being, i.e., between theological discourse and a universal horizon.

We are thus left searching for a way beyond this back and forth between TP and TO, a way that allows us to avoid the choice between the mutually exclusive options of either articulating a unity of theological discourse and ontological discourse or asserting the particularity of signification against any universalizing horizon. Immanence provides this way with its reciprocally constitutive distinction of signification and namelessness. This is to say, once again, that it is necessary both to signify immanence excessively and to maintain the proper namelessness of the ontological immanence that is variously signified. What corresponds to this dual necessity is an affirmation both of particular signification and of a horizon—the nameless ontological immanence—that traverses these various particular significations. Because there are only relays between immanence's namelessness and its significations, neither pole can become prior to the other. Consequently, it must be said that TO fails when it attends to the relation, left in abeyance by TP, between theological discourse and being, for in doing so it does not conceive the *distinction* between signification and namelessness. Theological discourse must articulate a relation to being, but it cannot meet this demand by simply contending that God and being are convertible, and this is due to the simple reason that being is nameless. It is necessary to signify being, but no signification—even that of God—is proper to being. The severance of being and God, which was effected by Scotus and innovated by Heidegger, poses an irreproachable opposition to TO's desire to render them convertible. Ontological discourse and theological discourse remain exterior to, and thus distinguishable from, one another—though this is not to say, as TP does, they are unrelated. Immanence, by understanding the God expressed in theological discourse as an excessive signification of a properly nameless ontological dimension, provides a way to affirm this distinction-in-relation without resorting to TO's positing of convertibility. The approach of immanence has, additionally, the advantage of highlighting the contingency and impropriety of theological discourse, thus preserving the value of other manners of signification.

The fourth paradigm is one of "Philosophical Excess" (PE). This paradigm resembles most closely that of PD, for PE has no interest in affirming—at least not in any immediate or auto-referential manner—theological discourse. The endeavor remains one of philosophy. There is, however, a significant difference between these two paradigms. PD, I have noted, seeks to circumscribe and evaluate theological discourse from the outside, but PE maintains a degree of suspicion about the feasibility of such an operation. If PD addresses theological discourse by means of circumscription, then PE addresses it by means of contamination. This is to say that PE retains an awareness of the way in which a philosophical overcoming of theological discourse is not entirely successful—philosophy remains contaminated by theological discourse. PE does not then jettison the aim of a purely philosophical project, rather it seeks to fulfill such an aim by returning to this contamination. The aim of philosophy becomes contingent on a rethinking of theological contamination, a rethinking that is at once a dispelling of the theological and a renewal of philosophy. Theological contamination thus engenders a paraphilosophical discourse that forms a pivot for an intrinsically philosophical advance.

The variants of this paradigm are quite diverse, moreso than with other paradigms. Accordingly, even as they share the same interest, broadly conceived, it is worth naming several contemporary instances: Jacques Derrida, who remained intrigued by the logic of a certain messianicity; Giorgio Agamben, who has, in addition to his own interrogation of the messianic, addressed the question of political theology in many variations; Slavoj Žižek, who has invoked Christianity as an ally for his own Hegelo-Lacanian version of Marxist philosophy; Jean-Luc Nancy, who recognizes a demand for the deconstruction of Christianity; and Alain Badiou, who, in order to demonstrate the relation between his central concepts of subject, event, and fidelity, turned to Paul. What is common to these instances is not the precise value given to theological discourse, for that varies according to the specific interests of each philosopher. It is, rather, the refusal to grasp theological discourse as something utterly foreign in nature to philosophical production. Again, this does not mean theological discourse is to be accommodated, but it does mean that philosophy, in order to fulfill its own endeavors, must think through or make use of its imbrication with theological discourse.

This paradigm is particularly interesting for immanence, insofar as PE is able to bring into focus the peculiar distinction-in-relation of philosophical and theological discourse. Of course, there is a sense in which PD, TP, and TO all acknowledge the differential tension between ontological and theological registers of thought—but the response of these paradigms to such differential tension is to resolve it. The tension functions as a motor of development for a paradigm of resolution. The precise ways in which this tension is resolved will diverge, running from a philosophical regulation of theology (PD), to a theological refusal of philosophy (TP), to an identification of theology and philosophy (TO), yet in each case there is ultimately some kind of resolution. What is therefore interesting about PE is that such a resolution is not provided—or if it is, it is not foregrounded. The issue at hand, then, becomes one of the *problematic* character of the differential tension, given that resolutions have thus far proved premature.[19]

Immanence affirms PE's emphasis on the problematic character of the relation between philosophy and theological discourse—though immanence would, once again, address this problematic character in terms of namelessness and signification. It is often the case that an advance resides not in its synthetic power but in its destructive capacity. This is what happens with PE, the prominence of which lies in its ability to disrupt a straightforward philosophical overcoming of theological discourse (though it equally disrupts the endeavors of TP and TO). PE clears a field of possibility by showing what is no longer possible. The ways, then, in which exemplars of PE begin to articulate the relation of philosophy and theological discourse will be less important than the problematic they highlight. These articulations, in fact, tend to be ad hoc in nature, and if there is a notable weakness in PE then it lies in its silence with regard to a consistent theoretical approach for addressing this problematic. The ontological register and the theological register operate according to different modalities, and the achievement of PE is to make this difference a condition of thought. What then becomes necessary, however, is to think these modalities—in their difference, of course, but also in their relation. Immanence makes its agreement with PE into an occasion for going beyond PE, and it does this by thinking the differential tension of a philosophical, or ontological, register (namelessness) and a theological register (signification) as mutually constitutive, or as relays of one another.

---

19. A more precise account of the sense and import that I give to the "problematic" will be provided in the following chapter.

Surplus Naming

PE can thus be distinguished from the other three paradigms in virtue of its awareness of an indeterminacy circulating throughout the relation between philosophy and theological discourse. There is a truth to be grasped in this indeterminacy, though it requires a degree of conceptual articulation not provided by PE. What is this truth? It is that philosophical and theological discourses belong to something that, while expressed by each of them, is prior to them. They share, in other words, a common condition. Accordingly, the fundamental task of thought becomes one of thinking this common condition—or, more precisely, of thinking the commonality as it is differentially expressed by philosophy and theological discourse (for the commonality is not something positive that transcends them). There is an indeterminate relation of philosophy and theological discourse because they belong to an immanent surplus that is both nameless and in need of signification. Any attempt to properly name this surplus, to make it immanent *to* something, will generate a primary discourse and its remainder, and thus a relation between a transcendent point of reference and an excess that departs from this transcendence. The immanence of surplus is obviously denied by the introduction of the transcendent, yet there is a further consequence that must be noted: surplus is no longer primary, it is no longer that which enables the simultaneous production of philosophical discourse on the nameless and of theological discourse's signification. There is no longer any differential tension of namelessness and signification, of philosophy and theological discourse, for one has achieved a prominence that allows it to derivatively position the other.

Surplus must function as the common condition of philosophy and theology—a commonality that is expressed in their differential tension, which is intrinsic to the immanence of signification and namelessness, of God and Nature. This, however, is lost with the presumptions of the transcendent in PD, TP, and TO. Surplus, in these, is no longer the excessive, productive differential between philosophy and theology, for it gets coded and thus regulated according to the prior relations established by the discourse that presumes to be transcendent. For immanence, these relations are derivative and the surplus is primary—even though this synchronic primacy must be expressed through the diachronic fecundity of relays between namelessness and signification. It can therefore be said that the most grievous failure of transcendence, as it is found in PD, TP, and TO, is that it cuts itself off from surplus production, or from the differential relays of philosophy and theological discourse. These three paradigms take one moment in a diachronic series of relays and make it into a point of reference that transcends the very movement that conditions them. It is for this reason, then, that immanence, in critically assaying them, is able to pose them against one another: if each paradigm grasps some moment in the series of relays, then it is possible to make each paradigm into an illuminating point of reference on the others. Nonetheless, it is inadequate to try to piece these moments together into a larger series. Far more beneficial is the attempt to think the conditions of the movement of which they are moments—this is not only because of the obvious advantage that thought of conditions has over thought of the conditioned, but also because only in this way are we able to understand the nature of the indeterminacy that makes possible the alternation from one moment to another. After all, it must be confessed that the indeterminacy that haunts and virtually destabilizes each paradigm is never conceived—at least not in its constitutive power to generate the philosophy/theology differential—by any of these paradigms. On the contrary, each paradigm seeks to subject any indeterminacy to its own logic. The only possible exception to this statement is PE, insofar as it foregrounds the failure of PD and seeks to rethink philosophy's relation to theological discourse.

What I am suggesting, then, is that immanent surplus should be understood as the "reverse cause" of the paradigms of PD, TP, and TO.[20]

20. The character and implications of reverse causality are variegated and wide-ranging, so I should make clear what my intention is in drawing on this term. Specifically, I am interested in the way in which a cause may be understood not as being actually present, but instead as being that in relation to which the present actualizes itself, even as it appears to be absent from the present. In this regard, I have been deeply influenced by Kenneth Surin's discussion, in *Freedom Not Yet*, of reverse causality in the context of communism (or heterotopia) and capitalism. According to Surin, we should locate causality not in capitalism but in communism, the fear of which causes capitalism to be what it is. "In the case of the political domain, the action of a reverse cause takes place when some ostensibly 'future' state of affairs, the communist revolution, say, is warded off in the present by the forces that keep capitalism in place. . . . Capitalism is what it is precisely because it has to be organized in such a way that it can keep at bay those forces which, if they are not weakened or dissolved by already existing capitalism, would bring about the communist revolution. The revolution, which is yet to occur, is already active as a reverse cause that already existing capitalism has to contend with, and dispel with some success, if capitalism is to continue to exist" (217). What I am suggesting by way of analogy, then, is that the rival paradigms under critique may be understood as

Accounts of causation usually rely upon a given, fixed point of reference (in either the present or the past), which then becomes that which enables the selection of one possibility from a set of many possibilities; it is the cause of the effect realized by this selection. The limit of this sort of approach, from the vantage of reverse causality, is that it cannot think the pre-referential background of what is determined as cause and effect (i.e., the background against which points of reference are determined). Such an approach appears—again, from the vantage of reverse causality—to begin with given determinants, to then conceive the link of necessity between them, but all the while to leave out of consideration the possibility that these determinants are determined not within themselves, but rather against a background that never appears as given. In other words, it may be the case that causality proceeds not by way of the selection of one out of many determinate possibilities, but rather in virtue of an awareness of and a concomitant attempt to ward off a possibility that never appears among the determinate possibilities. (In fact, it may be the case that the appearance of the set of possibilities is determined by the attempt to ward off a possibility that must remain inapparent.) Reverse causation affirms such a suspicion, for it asserts that the cause (let us call it A) is determined by its attempt to ward off a possibility (let us call it X). In this instance, then, X would be the reverse cause of A. Or, to put it more precisely, it can be said that the movement from A to B—in which the causality opposed by reverse causality would discern A as cause of the effect B—is caused by X, i.e., by A's desire to prevent X from being realized. Therefore it would be mistaken to say that B is the effect of A. Rather, B is the effect of A's encounter with an X that it wishes to preclude from realization; B is caused not by A, but instead by A's refusal of X (where B names a determination that allows A to successfully evade the selection of X).

This brief sketch of reverse causality can be usefully applied to the problematic relation of philosophy and theology—that is, to the critique I am presenting, from the vantage of immanence, of the regnant paradigms seeking to address this problematic. The surplus of immanence, in its constitutive differential of namelessness and signification, is not only the condition of possibility for these paradigms, it is also that which these paradigms seek to ward off. Immanent surplus is, in short,

---

being determined by their refusal of a future in which an immanent relay between the philosophical and the theological (or the religious) would be affirmed. It is precisely such a future that this book seeks to conceive.

the reverse cause of these paradigms. Reverse causation is especially illuminating here because it allows us to conceive a condition that remains
immanent to what it conditions. This is to say that immanence can be
understood—rightly, according to my argument—as that which is prior
to the determination offered by these paradigms, but it can do so without
ever having to appear as positively determined, i.e., as something that,
in itself, transcends these paradigms. It is for this reason that surplus
appears as the *immanent* excess of a paradigm's specific determination.
What thus becomes important is not to envision some perfected immanence in itself, prior to determination, but rather to make the excess of
these paradigms into a pathway for the re-expression of surplus. Only in
this way is the relay of namelessness and signification, which is cut off by
the transcendent points of reference set forth by these rival paradigms,
re-opened. It is in virtue of this criterion that PE may be distinguished
from PD, TP, and TO, for unlike them it foregrounds the instability of
philosophical-theological indeterminacy. PE seeks, in other words, to
release the excess of determination—figured here as philosophical-theological indeterminacy—from its hegemonic points of reference. Surplus,
rather than becoming overcoded by the strictures of a paradigm, becomes
decoded, shifting, and thus capable of relay.

What is necessary, beyond PE, is to begin to think this surplus constructively. Surplus must cease to be the reverse cause, or that which is
warded off, and must instead become that which is affirmed. Of course,
it is not possible simply to affirm surplus, for it is immanent to its ex-
pressions (even as it exceeds them)—it is, in fact, not simple but instead
differentially constituted by namelessness and signification. It comes into
view as the constitutive background of the paradigms that ward it off.
Indeed, despite the disagreements of these paradigms, they all agree on
what must be warded off (or, in the case of PE, on what is only vaguely
grasped), and this is an immanent surplus that is constructively expressed
as the relay between the distinct yet mutually constitutive necessities of
namelessness and signification.

In order to give a more exact sense of what it means to affirm an
immanent surplus that is expressed by means of relay, I will now turn to
Spinoza, who is, of course, a central figure for any thought of immanence.
As I have already proposed, Spinoza's denomination of immanence—or
of what he calls substance—as "God, or Nature" is one that should be
maintained in its duality. This is to say that neither should be understood

as a rhetorical code whose authentic meaning is given by the other term. This is rather uncontroversial with regard to the claim that Nature really refers to God—after all, the claim that substance and its modes are immanent contravenes the transcendence of an ontologically distinct deity. More to the point, however, my insistence on reading "God, or Nature" as an immanent duality stands against the presumption that God is dispensable insofar as Nature is the true referent of immanence. To discard God in this manner is to discard signification, and this cannot be done—not because signification (or God) furnishes us with immanence's proper name (it does not, for immanence is nameless), but because the production of signification, even in its improper fictionality, is necessitated by immanence. I am now able to add that "God, or Nature" encapsulates, at the synchronic level, the relay between signification and namelessness, which is to say the indeterminacy of immanence that functions as reverse cause of the paradigms of the philosophical-theological relation that I have considered.

A brief adumbration of the approach Spinoza takes to the appropriation and preclusion of theological discourse, in relation to his philosophy of immanence, can help indicate in greater detail what it would mean to install the sort of relay I am advancing. This adumbration relies on the particular interpretation of Spinoza proposed by Yirmiyahu Yovel—an interpretation, it may be said, that is but one among many. The observation that there are many Spinozas may appear as a banality; it is nonetheless observed in order to mark my awareness that it is possible to propose other interpretations of Spinoza, which may be at variance with my interests. In turning to Yovel, then, my aim is not to enter into contestation over the "true" interpretation of Spinoza. It is, more precisely, to further develop the paradigm I am advancing. Yovel's interpretation, in other words, peculiarly illumines an aspect of Spinoza that is in concord with the theoretical aims I take to be central to immanence, and to the consistent thinking of immanence's consequences for theological discourse.

Yovel's interpretation of Spinoza echoes my own most explicitly in his refusal to see Spinoza as abandoning the question of God, or more generally of theological discourse. According to the interpretation I am opposing, immanence would require a thoroughgoing rejection not only of transcendence, but also of every signification that can be connected to the God that happens to be imagined as transcendent. This utter rejection, however, is precisely what Spinoza refuses to propose.

> Although Spinoza secularizes religion, he also creates a system of naturalist rationalism which preserves some of the supreme goals of the historical religions it rejects. It is therefore essential to Spinoza that the semireligious dimension of philosophy not be shed along with the many errors and superstitions that have governed it in the past. Spinoza's philosophy is also concerned with God, or the absolute, and the soul's identification with it; and ultimately it aspires to wisdom and a new form of salvation.[21]

What Yovel asks us to imagine, then, is something that is neither purely naturalistic nor identifiable with a theology of the transcendent. Spinoza's endeavor is philosophical, for it is generated by thought's attempt to think the world apart from any prior transcendent condition. The danger in this endeavor, however, is that the rejection of transcendence may come to entail the rejection of an authentically philosophical aim, which involves the desire to think the absolute, to achieve wisdom, and to conceive salvation (or liberation). The paradox, then, is that the authentically philosophical aim cannot be maintained if philosophy defines itself by means of an a priori rejection of theological discourse. There is a "semireligious" dimension of philosophy that must be preserved in spite of and within the philosophical rejection of transcendence. Accordingly, while there is a secularizing impulse involved in immanence, it is a secularity that overlaps with the very theological discourse from which it departs— "God, or Nature."

Crucially, the space in which it becomes possible to imagine this thing that is neither reductive naturalism nor theological transcendence is the space of signification. As Yovel observes, "some of the major drives that had in the past animated religion and even mysticism are still partly at work within Spinoza's naturalist rationalism," and thus we find Spinoza "using some of the old vocabulary."[22] What are some of these names? According to Yovel, instances may be found with "*pietas, religio*, or *salus*."[23] Once again, we should resist the temptation to understand these names as so many ruses—indeed, "such terms as 'God' and its derivatives are used in earnest."[24] Spinoza thus serves as an excellent exemplar of the approach I am advancing, one in which the opposition of immanence to

21. Yovel, *Spinoza and Other Heretics*, 148.
22. Ibid.
23. Ibid., 137.
24. Ibid.

transcendence requires not the rejection of theological discourse's signi-fication, but on the contrary a renewed expression of it. Of course, these names function differently, for they no longer properly represent the transcendent. Nonetheless, through their relay they re-express the desires heretofore captured in the transcendent by newly orienting them around immanence. What we are left with is nothing more and nothing less than a relay between immanence's namelessness and its necessary significa-tion. If the former calls for secularization, the latter can be seen as a kind of sacralization. These tendencies relay one another, they belong to an immanent circulation that is never finally profane or sacred, naturalistic or religious. We may again refer to Yovel: "Spinoza can be seen also as secularizing religion without giving up its absolute pathos, or as sacral-izing reason by giving it the supreme spiritual tasks that were wrongly attributed to religious mysticism."[25]

I have thus far focused on the role of signification, but my argument also bears an ontological dimension. Immanence, ontologically speaking, names a reality that rejects any transcendent beyond, but it does so from a point prior to the distinction between a beyond and a below. What imma-nence defends, in other words, must not be defined by a prior relation to the beyond. According to the false picture set up by the prior relation, the affirmation of immanence amounts to the severance of the world from a beyond. What is thus missed is that the world, for immanence, has a reality that cannot submit to this distinction of a beyond and a below. Immanence means the mere below, cut off from the beyond, only if we first accept an ontology of transcendence—but immanence involves, at its heart, a thoroughgoing rejection of this ontology. To affirm immanence is not to affirm the below against the beyond, it is to refuse such an op-position. This, of course, is the reason Spinoza speaks of "God, or Nature": to simply pose Nature *against* God would be to accept the terms already initiated by an ontology of transcendence. As Yovel points out, "Spinoza does not contend that there is no God, only the inferior natural world. Such a contention is itself steeped in a Christian world view." [26] The way to evade a transcendent ontology, then, lies in relay, in undoing the opposed realms of being by way of their immanent intertwining. The beyond is already below, but this means that the below includes what the beyond

25. Ibid., 37–38.
26. Ibid., 175.

made separate. Following this logic, Yovel is able to claim that "Spinoza contends . . . that by virtue of identifying the world with God, immanent reality itself acquires divine status."[27]

At this point, we face the crude yet indicative question of how we are to locate Spinoza's work. It cannot finally be situated within religious discourse insofar as it insists on a philosophically developed account of immanence, but neither can it be finally situated within philosophy insofar as it maintains certain directives signified by religious discourse. I would suggest, with an eye towards the following chapter's discussion of diaspora, that Spinoza's straddling of the divide between philosophy and religion, or between secular namelessness and fictive signification, is not unrelated to the complex religio-cultural hybridity of his historical circumstances. He was, first of all, a Jew, which is to say that he was never monolingual but always already in between many languages. "What," Yovel remarks, "was Spinoza's language? In a word: he had none. Like many Jews, he was a polyglot, lacking a single language in which he was exclusively and genuinely at home and which dominated his life and semantic universe."[28] For one in such a situation, the fictive and excessive character of signification can more easily be seen as a starting point, an irreducible datum, rather than something to be reconciled into a higher unity of transcendental meaning. The differential nature of Spinoza's relation to signification leads, furthermore, to a differential account of his relation to culture—as Yovel continues, "Nor was there a single society to which he belonged."[29] Along these lines, Yovel makes much of Spinoza's status as a Marrano. Without necessarily giving as much weight as Yovel does to the ability of this fact to function as a cipher for the entirety of Spinoza's work, it can certainly be granted that the Marrano's peculiarly diasporic status is more than incidental to the peculiarly interstitial character of Spinoza's philosophico-religious thought. As Yovel observes, "Wherever he turns, the Marrano is an outsider and someone 'new' (he is a New Christian or a New Jew). He does not belong to any cultural context simply or naturally, and feels both inside and outside any one of them."[30] What Spinoza's historical context might indicate, then, is the potential connection between the differentiality of immanence—as both nameless and excessively signified—and the

27. Ibid.
28. Ibid., 173–74.
29. Ibid.
30. Ibid., 49.

differentiality of cultural diaspora. This ability to be simultaneously inside and outside is central to the production of the new, or to the differential composition at work in diaspora. It is, in fact, this diasporic differentiality that must now be given attention.

2

Diaspora

And if you greet only your brothers and sisters, what more are
you doing than others? Do not even Gentiles do the same?

—Jesus[1]

Counterposing Christianity

CENTRAL TO CHRISTIANITY IS its gospel, which is better understood in
its more literal translation as "good news" (*euangelion*). Christianity,
at least in principle, is inseparable from the declaration of a novel con-
figuration of reality, as well as from the consequent demand not simply
to accept the abstract veracity of this declaration's content, but moreso to
enact it. What then is this content? It seems, minimally, to involve the love
of enemies and the human imitation of divine perfection—the command
to "Love your enemies" (Matt 5:44) is soon followed by the injunction to
"Be perfect, therefore, as your heavenly Father is perfect" (Matt 5:48)—as
well as the forgiveness of debts and the liberation from slavery (or more
broadly from structures of power that oppress).[2] The Jubilee-inspired
link between economic and socio-political liberation is stressed, among

---

1. Matt 5:47.

2. My selection of texts in this paragraph largely follows the selection made by John
Howard Yoder in *Nonviolence*, 85–91, which itself is an adumbration of his argument for
the irreducibly political character of Jesus's life and preaching in *Politics of Jesus*.

other places, in Luke's account, which has Jesus introduce himself to the public by reading a prophecy that he claims to fulfill: "The Spirit of the Lord is upon me, because he has anointed me to bring good news to the poor. He has sent me to proclaim release to the captives and recovery of sight to the blind, to let the oppressed go free, to proclaim the year of the Lord's favor" (Luke 4:18–19). The same account has Mary proclaim of God: "He has brought down the powerful from their thrones, and lifted up the lowly; he has filled the hungry with good things, and sent the rich away empty" (Luke 1:52–53). Or again, as Jesus says, "many who are first will be last, and the last will be first" (Mark 10:31).[3] Christian declaration is anti-dominative—importantly, however, the liberation it offers is not only posed against the mode of domination, it is also posed on behalf of the construction of new social bonds or solidarities, the possibility of which is based upon the enactment of enemy-love. What is declared, then, is a rather fundamental refusal of pre-established (political, social, and economic) relations not only "vertically," whereby those above are overthrown by those below, but also "horizontally," whereby the strict disjunction of friend and enemy is undone by the practice of a divinely perfect love.[4] The good news is that all of this is possible insofar as the messianic kingdom has arrived.

Such a Christian declaration tends to conflict with one's normal experience of the world. The obviousness of such an observation should not undermine its importance. Nonetheless, what is of more immediate interest for the questions I am here pursuing is another observation,

3. It may be noted, in view of my argument (further on in this chapter) that Christian declaration can be understood so as to cut against any sedimentation of Christian identity, that this reversal also seems to apply to attempts to constitute a stable power structure in Jesus's kingdom. For instance, when James and John ask Jesus for privileged positions of superiority in his kingdom—"to sit, one at your right hand and one at your left" (Mark 10:37)—Jesus launches into a disquisition that Mark narratively encapsulates by having Jesus say that "whoever wishes to become great among you must be your servant, and whoever wishes to be first among you must be slave of all" (Mark 10:44). This kingdom is meant to be different in character from those found elsewhere, "among the Gentiles," where it is the case that "their rulers lord it over them, and their great ones are tyrants over them" (Mark 10:42). It is as if one has to give up the desire to have what has been previously recognized as a kingdom—or, as I will suggest in this chapter, a territorialized identity—in order to enact what Jesus declares.

4. It is precisely insofar as such enemy-love is intertwined with an antagonistic relation to established power—an intertwining, in other words, between what I have called the "horizontal" and the "vertical"—that we can resist the temptation to equate it with a depoliticized tolerance.

one that focuses less on the conflict between Christian declaration and one's normal experience of the world and more on the conflict between Christian declaration and the history of Christianity's performance of this declaration. This is to say that even though Christian declaration may appear incredible, the barrier erected by this incredibility is mediated through exposure to the performance of the declaration. If Christian declaration remains barricaded within itself, this is a result not so much of its abstractly apparent incredibility as of its having become discredited by dint of its performance. Thus, the basic question to be posed with regard to Christianity is not its divergence from the world but rather its divergence from itself, its failure to be performed in a way that renders persuasive what it has declared. To put it simply, and perhaps too mildly, Christianity's historical performance has not proceeded in accord with the content of its declaration. Since its good news has often, in fact, amounted to bad news, it is not at all difficult to counterpose Christian performance to Christian declaration. My aim in this chapter, however, is not to put this counterposition in service of an essential rebuttal of Christianity, nor is it to somehow save the Christian declaration by severing it from its historical performance. It is instead to think the conditions of possibility *for* this counterposition, which is to say the conditions that enable us to counterpose declaration and historical performance.

The thesis I wish to pursue is that this counterposition of Christian declaration and Christian performance is made possible by Christianity's lack of a concept of diaspora. It is better to say "lack" rather than "refusal," for the latter would imply that the initial essence of Christianity was diasporic, and that at some later point this diasporic character was refused. There may be some truth to this account of an historical refusal, but the possible advantages of such an account are outweighed by a prominent disadvantage, which is that the account of an historical refusal allows us to divide a pristine, Edenic original Christianity from its historical corruption. Christianity is thus provided with an alibi, for even as it takes responsibility for its failures it coevally secures its claim to something transcending these failures. There are many articulations of this alibi, and they usually proceed by demarcating a fundamental scission between a pure pole and a corrupted pole: Jesus and Paul, idea and history, primitive and institutional, and so on. These scissions are to be lauded for their attempt to think the obvious disjunction between Christian declaration and performance, but they must simultaneously be rejected due to the fact that, in order to think this disjunction, they fall back on a rather cumbersome essentialism. We are always told that the scission belongs to the perversion of an essence that, having been lost, must now be recovered—which is to say that awareness of Christianity's historical failure, oddly enough, restores the criterion of Christianity. Accordingly, even if it may very well be the case that diaspora was, once upon a time, a commitment entailed by Christianity, it is better not to become invested in this possibility. This is because such an investment makes us servants to the task of saving Christianity from itself, of espying a Christian essence that, even as it is counterposed by the history of Christianity, cannot be affected by this counterposition. In such a scenario, to think the discrediting of Christian declaration by Christian performance is to think the eternal viability of Christian declaration. This, I think it is fair to say, puts us within a vicious circle.

My aim, then, is to propose a diasporic account of Christianity without simultaneously claiming that this diasporic Christianity accords with some ahistorical essence of Christianity. In other words, even as I hope to render compelling a vision of Christianity as diasporic, I am not claiming that this vision agrees with the "true" version of Christianity. After all, who, or what, is able to provide this "true" version? There is, once again, no essence of Christianity to be recovered, and this means, furthermore, that there is no essence of Christianity to bless or curse once and for all. The interest of a diasporic account of Christianity is not to understand the essence of Christianity; it is instead to understand the conditions that enable the counterposition of Christian performance and declaration. I am arguing, in other words, that it is the lack of a concept of diaspora that enables the history of Christianity to assert its filiation—either positively or negatively—from Christian declaration. By proposing a diasporic account of Christianity I am not only conceiving this strange evolution from declaration to counterpositional historical performance, I am also resisting its explanatory finality. This is, of course, to turn Christian declaration against Christian performance, but not in such a way that Christianity would be preserved; for there is no claim that Christianity was, once upon a time, diasporic. The interest therefore is not to save an authentic Christianity from its corruption but rather to change the way we think about and contextualize Christianity; it is not to return Christianity to its authentic diasporic essence but rather to use diaspora as a vantage by which one style of approaching Christianity (and this includes those approaches that rely on a scission between the authentic and the corrupt) can be deposed and another can be imagined.

Such an interest is in accord with the theory of immanence that I developed in the previous chapter. There it was argued that even as an immanence insists on the proper namelessness of being, it also insists on the excessive, improper signification that is produced with the same necessity by which being remains nameless. Any discourse on Christianity, then, should be understood as an instance of this signification that is both improper to the namelessness of immanence and constructively expressive of the very same immanence. To think Christianity is not to think the proper name of being, but neither is it to think something epiphenomenal to the real (and this last is especially the case insofar as the signification engendered by Christianity has prominently influenced history). Consequently, what is at stake is not referential adequacy to an authentic Christianity. It is instead an innovative—which is to say differentially repetitive rather than referentially adequate—negotiation concerned not only with the signification that Christianity has produced, but also with the signification that Christianity might become able to produce. Mary-Jane Rubenstein, in reflecting on the contemporary relationship between Christianity and global capitalism, has observed the apparently dichotomous potential of Christian signification by observing that the "task is . . . to account for the emergence of this profound split at the heart of a tradition: how is it that a certain heritage of Christianity has forged the paths of globalization by means of political and economic imperialism, while another maintains Christianity's anti-materialism, anti-colonialism and communitarianism?"[5] The undecidability of Christianity's relation to the dominant social, political, and economic paradigm of the present points to a more fundamental undecidability within Christianity itself. This undecidability is unsurprising for a theory of immanence, given that such a theory understands Christianity in terms of excessive, improper signification. From this vantage Christianity ceases to revolve around a true essence to which various and mutually exclusive Christianities would competitively lay claim. Christianity becomes, on the contrary, a serially produced fiction, one that can never be traced back to its origin, one that can only be produced again and again. The conception of Christianity in virtue of diaspora is precisely such a production.

5. Rubenstein, "Capital Shares," 105.

The Problematic of Form

Christian declaration, as it is pronounced and enacted by Jesus, concerns a possibility of immanent existence. It will be protested, no doubt, that this is not the case, insofar as Jesus declares the will of a God that is transcendent—and it is true, this is one way to understand Christian declaration. As I have remarked, however, there are many ways to understand Christian declaration, and so while it is reasonable to understand this declaration in terms of transcendence, it is likewise feasible to pursue an immanent understanding. The value of an immanent understanding becomes particularly relevant if, as I will propose, a transcendent understanding is what promotes the separation of declaration from historical performance. An additional advantage of an immanent understanding, and one more germane to my immediate concern, is that it allows us to foreground a prominent, though often underemphasized, aspect of Christian declaration—namely, that it is antagonistically positioned.

This is to say that it is difficult to understand Christian declaration without understanding its rather explicit antagonism towards the world as it is presently determined. Thus, while it is possible to make Christian declaration into a discourse on the nature of being, one can do so only by a flagrant decontextualization. Christian declaration is not fundamental ontology; it is instead an articulation of a possibility of existence that is precluded, or determined as unrealistic, by the present organization of existence. To prise Christian declaration from such an antagonistic context is to fail to take seriously this declaration's force. Christian declaration is no doubt for the world, the only one we have, but it is also against this world, insofar as this world is presently determined so as to remain inhospitable to the actual performance of what is declared. How can Christian declaration be for this world if it is simultaneously against this world's refusal of it? We find ourselves in precisely such a paradox once we take ourselves outside of Christian declaration's antagonistic context, once we make it into a directly ontological discourse, once we depoliticize it in the name of being—or, more to the point, in the name of the transcendent. John Howard Yoder, for instance, observes the link between transcendence and the removal of antagonism from Christian declaration when he claims that "patterns" of thought that depoliticize Jesus all "relegate our response to Jesus' call to love the enemy to some other plane of reality than the real world."[6] This, then, is the advantage of an immanent understanding of Christian declaration: since immanence consists of nothing other than its constructive expression, there is no ontological place that can transcendently preserve this gospel outside of the context in which it is declared and performed. There is no point from which the antagonism of Christian declaration can be transcended, no way of affirming this declaration outside of the antagonism that it encounters or engenders (and this is not because it refuses the world, but precisely because it affirms the world). Christian declaration concerns nothing more and nothing less than the effectuation of a possibility of existence—yet to understand it in terms of transcendence is to install its effectuation at a level beyond, and unaffected by, the endeavor to perform this possibility.

The possibility of existence Jesus declares is therefore an oppositional discourse. It cannot be a straightforward theory of being due to the simple fact that what it opposes—or what opposes it—*does* exist. Christian declaration is thus a discourse on what may be, not on what is—it concerns becoming rather than being, possibilities of existence rather than what has already actualized its own existence. An ontology compatible with Christian declaration must therefore be one that can account not only for the possibilities of existence declared by Jesus, but also for the possibilities of existence opposed by Jesus's declaration. A theory of immanence, it should be noted, meets these requirements: its proper namelessness renders both Christian declaration and opposition to Christian declaration improper; its affirmation of excessive signification makes conceivable both the Christian possibilities of existence and the possibilities of existence that Christian declaration opposes. What matters is not an articulation of some correspondence between Christian declaration and being, but rather an articulation of the antagonistic nature of Christian declaration.

It is therefore mistaken to imagine that features of the Christian declaration, such as enemy-love or liberation from oppression, can be separated from the antagonism they encounter from, and that they pose against, the structures of existence that refuse such directives. The declaration is "good news" only insofar as it is able to stand against the regnant patterns of existence. Any suspicion about the importance of such antagonism is ultimately quelled when we note that the one who makes

---

6. Yoder, *Nonviolence*, 91.

the declaration is killed by "the Powers" that remain in opposition.[7] Yet the fact that Jesus does not respond to his death sentence with violence should not be understood as a diminution of antagonism, or some kind of masochistic détente. The crucifixion retains the antagonism of Christian declaration; it is just that it includes, as part of this declaration, the refusal of violence as a means of antagonism, or the refusal of the terms set forth by the Powers that are resisted.

What all of this forces us to consider is the impossibility of separating the content of Christian declaration from its formal relation to what it opposes, or to what opposes it. Content cannot be severed from the formal antagonism it engenders (though one can say, counterfactually, that antagonism would cease if the world became favorably disposed towards the content of the declaration). How, then, are we to conceive this formal antagonism? This is a central question, given that the devaluation of antagonism enables a dilution of content. What is necessary, in order to forestall this process of devaluation and diminution, is not a compensatory affirmation of violence. This is out of the question, given Jesus's own refusal to respond in kind to the violence set upon him by his antagonists. It is incumbent upon us to conceive a form of antagonism that, while remaining truly antagonistic, does not rely on a violence that is symbolically oppositional or instrumentally justified by a reification of the good (adherents of Christian declaration) and the evil (opponents of Christian declaration).

I am proposing, as a response to this demand, that we conceive Christian declaration as having a *problematic* form. The antagonism engendered by the content of Christian declaration should be understood in terms of the problematic. But what is the problematic? First of all, it is not a judgment made upon the Christian declaration, or on what opposes it, as the common academic usage—"I find that to be problematic"— would have it. To be problematic is not to be lacking in adequacy. The problematic is a mode of existence; it is not a predicate of judgment but an active mode of relating. To say that the form of Christian declaration is problematic is to say that affirmation of this declaration can proceed only in the mode of becoming, only by actively problematizing. Christian declaration has an irreducibly antagonistic relation to what refuses it, but this antagonism is not a strict opposition between two identities. It is bet-

---

7. A fuller account of "the Powers" is provided in chapter 3.

ter to say that Christian declaration poses a problem for the given modes of existence. Christian declaration does not oppose these modalities except by affirming possibilities that are inadmissible by them. It does not transcend the determination of the world that refuses it, nor does it submit to this determination. Instead, it proceeds *in the world* as a problematic horizon; it declares its content, and in doing so problematizes the world as it is presently given.

I have already adverted to the inelidable link between form and content in Christian declaration. This link can now be developed through the notion of the problematic. This is to say not only that the formal relation between Christian declaration and what opposes it is problematic—such that Christian declaration poses a problem for given modes of existence—but also that the content intrinsic to Christian declaration renders its self-expression problematic. The reason for this might best be exemplified through the directive of enemy-love, for to love an enemy is to love what is not the same as oneself. In order to adhere to the content of Christian declaration, one must exceed the form by which one identifies oneself. What then is the form of this declaration's content? It cannot be easily identified, for the content that belongs to the form requires, straightaway, the refusal of identifying forms. At the same time, this content cannot be formless in a pure sense, for to affirm such content requires the formation of positive relations. The content of enemy-love requires the refusal of form, but it also requires the construction of new forms—so how should we articulate these forms constructed by enemy-love? This question's force arises from the fact that what is constructed cannot be formless, but neither can it have a form that is analogous to the forms refused by enemy-love. It is necessary, in other words, both to affirm the construction of new forms of relation, intrinsic to the content of Christian declaration, and to articulate the nature of the constructed forms such that they do not resemble the nature of the very forms they refuse. The way to do this, I am proposing, is to understand the forms constructed by enemy-love as problematic in themselves. These constructed forms not only refuse the forms that reify friend and enemy, they also refuse their auto-sedimentation into the "Christian" form. The bonds formed by enemy-love problematize the forms of friend and enemy as well as their own final solidity.

It is important, in order to gain a sense of how it is possible for a problematic form to differ in nature from forms of identity, to highlight the intrinsically differential nature of the problematic.[8] Such a form is constituted by taking on various elements, and thus is something that emerges through a process of composition. A problematic form does not exist apart from this process by which elements that heretofore have belonged to different identity-forms are composed into new relations. A form is therefore problematic because it is fundamentally relational, such that these relations, by traversing the boundaries delineated by pre-existing forms of identification, present a problem for such boundaries. What distinguishes the problematic form is not that it is yet another form alongside the given forms, but rather that it fails to respect the boundaries of given forms. Elements that differ from one another—that belong to mutually exclusive identifying forms—enter into transversal relations that compose a new form. This new form, however, is distinct in nature from the given forms, and this is in virtue of its intrinsically differential character. *The declarative content of enemy-love does, then, engender forms, but these forms cannot be identified in advance; their form is nothing other than differential relations composed by the enactment of Christian declaration.* Yet this means that the differential nature of Christian declaration is a problem not only for the forms of power that refuse the content of Christian declaration, but also for the self-identity of Christianity. Christian declaration, by virtue of the same logic that allows it to actively problematize the world that opposes it, must also actively problematize itself. The form of Christian declaration is a variant one, and a radically variant one at that. It does not precede the elements that compose it, not even as an empty form; it is not an invariant that molds or receives the elements it includes. On the contrary, the form of Christian declaration consists of nothing more and nothing less than what it becomes capable of composing; it is differentially generated by whatever elements, brought together in enemy-love, enter into relation with one another.

Christianity, understood as that which is engendered by the content of Christian declaration, is problematic, or differential, through and through. If it poses a problem for the given forms of the world, it can only do so insofar as it problematizes its own form. Consequently, as soon as it undergoes a process of auto-sedimentation, whereby it gives itself a stable—which is to say unproblematic—form of identity, it ceases to pose a problem to the given world. Christianity then becomes something that

8. The provenance of the concept of the problematic, as I am using it, lies in Deleuze, *Difference and Repetition*, 214–79.

can be placed, something whose interests can be negotiated; the moment it becomes an invariant form, it can be conditioned by the forms that refuse the content of Christian declaration. The temptation to turn its irreducibility to given forms into a new, unproblematic form is one that shadows Christian declaration from the outset. Such a new form may be broader, perhaps more cosmopolitan, than the forms it opposed, but it will not preserve its antagonism to given forms as long as the character of its form resembles the character of the forms it opposes. Christianity, if it is to genuinely oppose the content of its declaration to that which refuses this content, cannot understand itself as a better form, but only as a different kind of form. What Christian declaration calls for is not a form transcending all other forms, but rather an immanent movement, problematically traversing these forms, that is bastard, impure, syncretic.

It will be beneficial, before advancing further, to note a few additional aspects of the immanent understanding of Christianity that I am proposing. First, I want to insist that the problematic character of Christianity contextualizes it within what is presently given. This does not mean that Christianity is limited to the contours of the given. What it does mean, though, is that Christianity cannot be imagined as something—as a substantive form—that emerges from, or belongs to, a context beyond the given. Christian declaration involves the active problematization of a field that it does not provide, much less possess. It is not limited by what is given, for it problematizes the given, but neither does it transcend the given, and this is precisely because it emerges problematically. Thus there is antagonism, but it is the antagonism of an immanently generated problem, not the antagonism between a transcendent beyond and a world that rejects this beyond.

Second, and following from the previous point, it must be maintained that the matter of Christian declaration is the same as the matter of what opposes it. This is to say that opposition occurs on the level of form rather than matter. The antagonism without which Christianity ceases to produce something different concerns, initially, the opposition between the content of Christian declaration and the Powers that refuse such content. Yet this antagonism takes place as the opposition between forms of identity, according to which the social field is organized, and the form of Christian declaration, which is differentially composed. It must not be overlooked, then, that this opposition at the level of form—and note that it is an opposition not between Christian and non-Christian forms, but rather between differential and identitarian forms—presupposes a commonality of matter. In fact, the inescapability of antagonism would be unimaginable if this were not the case, for Christian declaration can pose a threat only if it seeks to articulate that which is already being articulated by given forms. This may seem to state the obvious, but the point of this statement is to undermine the even more obvious assumption that Christianity must stand against the world. There is truth in this assumption only if it is recast, more abstrusely but more accurately, as follows: Christian declaration, because it calls for the production of differential forms, stands against the *forms* by which the world is presently given. Christianity is absolutely worldly, without reserve, insofar as the world names the matter of existence, the one and only substance. The antagonism it sets forth has nothing to do with being against the world, and everything to do with being against the forms according to which the world is determined so as to preclude the possibilities of existence—enemy-love, liberation—imagined by Christian declaration.

Third, we can assert that if Christianity is to be distinctive in any respect, then it will be in the way that it processes difference. There is no special substance possessed by Christianity and lacking outside of it. The distinctiveness of Christianity, if there is to be such a thing, lies in its declaration, which calls for a differential recomposition of the world. Of course, what opposes Christianity also deals with difference, but it does so in terms of identity, and it is on this very point that antagonism emerges. What Christian declaration opposes is the demand that the world be composed according to invariant forms. If Christianity is itself taken as an invariant form, then it ceases to pose any real difference. Its difference lies in its ability to affirm difference, to activate and adhere to the problematic. This, of course, is a contingent endeavor, one without guarantees of successful enactment. But the temptation to make Christianity into something invariant, perhaps because this sedimentation appears to give Christianity an integrity requisite to the antagonism it encounters, is one that forecloses even the possibility of an enactment that would be distinctive from what it opposes.

Discontinuity, Rupture, and Apocalyptic

Christianity, insofar as it seeks to construct differential forms of immanent existence, is irreducibly committed to discontinuity. Yet everything depends on how this discontinuity is conceived. There is certainly discontinuity—what I have called antagonism—between Christianity and what it opposes, but, importantly, this discontinuity is conditioned by Christianity's prior affirmation of its own discontinuity with itself, such that it is intrinsically discontinuous. It is the very character of Christianity, the content of its declaration, that is discontinuous; discontinuity emerges not as the interval between Christianity and its others, but rather as an intrinsically Christian task. This means that, for Christianity, discontinuity and integrity are not opposed, nor are they deployed in separate modalities—as is the case when discontinuity between Christianity and its others derives from Christianity's desire to preserve its integrity against the threat posed by these others. Affirmation of Christian declaration means affirmation of an existence that is discontinuous without reserve.

It would be mistaken to conceive of this discontinuity in terms of rupture, or irruption, and this is because rupture seems to imply the breaking-open of a self-enclosed domain from a point that lies outside of this domain. It is precisely this sense that is indicated by J. Louis Martyn's characterization of Christian apocalyptic as God's "invasive action."[9] I have remarked that antagonism must be situated at the level of form, as the opposition between differential and identitarian forms. The language of rupture, however, tends to preclude formal antagonism, placing it instead at the level of being—antagonism is ontologized, it is determined as that between the being of a rupturing transcendence and the being of a ruptured, because self-enclosed, domain. Against the irruption of transcendence, it must be affirmed that the world opposed by Christian declaration is not the being of the world, but the forms of identity that happen to govern the world. One may wish to rupture forms of identity, and in this way rupture indicates the negativity, the destructive force, involved in Christianity's antagonism. Yet it is difficult to see how rupture indicates the positivity, the constructive power, involved in the differential recomposition of that which is subjected to the forms that are the object of Christianity's antagonism. Rupture sets free, but it does not compose the matter that it liberates from what is ruptured—or if it does it can only do so by offering the liberated elements membership in a power that comes from outside the world.

9. Martyn, *Galatians*, 105.

The emergence of Christianity, of Christian declaration, is apocalyptic. The basic sense of this claim is that whatever may thus emerge should not be understood as maintaining continuity with what is already given, nor should it be understood as developing something implicit yet unpursued by what is already given. To be apocalyptic is to be different from, or fundamentally other than, the course that has been or is being set forth. In this sense, apocalyptic is radically futural. One way of addressing the nature of apocalyptic is to think of it in relation to history, where history is understood as providing the logic of continuity that is broken by apocalyptic. This history could be understood imperially as a history governed by some manner of sovereignty: to be historical here means to be included in—or to face exclusion in the name of—a domain from above. Yet this history of continuity need not only be seen as history from above; it could also be seen as history from within, where the continuity of history emerges not through sovereign exteriority but through historical interiority. Such a history would be teleological: the apparent diversity of historical expression is ultimately resolved, retrospectively, in the *telos* that was—or to put it more prophetically, will have been—developed by way of history. It is against the setting of such historical continuity (whether determined by sovereign outside or teleological inside) that the difference that emerges in apocalyptic becomes most perspicuous. To say that apocalyptic articulates discontinuity is to say that apocalyptic breaks open, or breaks down, historical continuity. This is its difference, and it is in virtue of this difference that it declares a future unthought by such history, a future that is to be constructed.

There is, of course, a degree of indeterminacy in these stipulations about apocalyptic. I have just noted the import of understanding the differential character of Christian declaration according to a logic of discontinuity. Yet, as I have also noted, apocalyptic has been thought quite unapologetically in terms of rupture. What I am calling for, then, is the imagination of apocalyptic such that it disengages from and explicitly stands against the conceptual denomination and implicit logic of rupture. This possibility may be advanced by briefly attending to the broader context of apocalyptic in which Jesus's gospel, and then Paul's thought, takes place.[10] Seth Schwartz, when addressing the historical emergence of apocalyptic, begins by making clear that he is "not interested in speculat-

10. A more extensive consideration of the relation between Pauline thought and apocalyptic will be offered in the following chapter.

ing about the origins of the narrative structure of apocalyptic mythology," since the "genetic problem seems insoluble."[11] Nonetheless, he asserts that its relatively sudden appearance requires explanation, and particularly one that does not rely on "straightforward evolutionary development."[12] There must have been something specific that called apocalyptic mythology—he refers to it primarily as "the Myth"—into prominence, such that it "first appears in writing in the third century B.C.E." and afterwards becomes "extremely common in Jewish literature and . . . of definitive importance for early Christians."[13] Why this sudden emergence? He argues that it should be placed within the context of covenant ideology's increasing ascendance in Jewish thought; the prominence of covenant ideology is what engenders the demand for what we now identify as apocalyptic. In the terms that I have been using, apocalyptic arises as a response to the *problematic* character of covenant ideology—that is, as a response to the inadequacy of this ideology to give sense to what happens.

The covenant ideology is one that believes in "God's absolute dependability to reward and punish as appropriate."[14] This means, Schwartz continues, that the cosmos is "a simple, well-ordered place—a cosmos in the literal sense. . . . In this view, then, the cosmic world is not riven by conflict and shaken by instability; it is thus devoid of drama and cannot be described by means of mythological narrative."[15] Such is the ideology that, as it gains influence, is called into question by apocalyptic, or more precisely that encounters problems that require the invention of something like apocalyptic. Obedience and reward do not appear to follow an orderly relation; the world demonstrates a kind of evil that seems to contravene the idea of a divine order. As Schwartz remarks, "God is not in control in any way."[16] How then is it possible, in the face of this sort of affective and intellectual experience, to continue to affirm the claims of the covenant?

11. Schwartz, *Imperialism and Jewish Society*, 75.

12. Ibid.

13. Ibid., 76.

14. Ibid., 65.

15. Ibid., 66.

16. Ibid., 78. He claims, further on, that "as a cosmology and an anthropology the covenant, for all its elegant simplicity (or rather because of it) was problematic. Life does not work the way the covenantal system says it should: God manifestly does not reward the righteous and punish the wicked, and Israel's observance of the covenant and performance of the cult does not guarantee its well-being" (83).

Apocalyptic, Schwartz observes, is an attempt to address this question in a rather nuanced manner, for it allows one to break with the evident limits of the covenant at the same time that one maintains a relation to the God with which one was heretofore covenantally related. In other words, apocalyptic provided a means by which ideas and affects unthought by the covenant could be expressed, but this resistance never actually effected an essential sundering in the self-understanding of those who pursued it. Apocalyptic served as the supplement of the covenant; Schwartz remarks that "though the systems are logically incongruous, they did not for the most part generate social division."[17] This is to say that the network of signification involved in covenant ideology was displaced by, and at the same time maintained in virtue of uneasy hybridization with, apocalyptic mythology. Yet the question of whether such hybridization is closer to innovation or compromise is not what interests me. More intriguing is the disjuncture (between covenant and apocalyptic) that logically precedes the evaluation of any subsequent hybridization. How, I am asking, are we to understand that process by which the coherence of signification involved in affirmation of covenant ideology breaks down?

There is more in reality than what the covenant signifies; there is something that exceeds the divinely ordered cosmos. The advantage of addressing apocalyptic in this manner is that it allows us to think more deeply, which is to say at the level of the condition of possibility, of what is signified in apocalyptic. We miss something when we simply observe that the signification of the covenant is replaced, or supplementarily displaced, by the signification of apocalyptic. However important this process may be, what remains more important is the dynamic at issue in this process—and this dynamic cannot be grasped by comparing and contrasting these significations, for when we do so we register the shift without attending to what enables the shift. Drawing on Schwartz's analysis, it becomes clear that what enables the shift is an affection and conceptualization of a world that slips between and extends beyond the boundaries signified by the covenantal ideology. This process, once again, is what I have called problematization. To insist on the problematic generation of apocalyptic is to call into awareness that apocalyptic, no matter what it signifies, is in its beginnings an immanent process—and this is because it is generated by an excess of the world. Apocalyptic thus becomes the signification of

17. Ibid., 81.

an immanent excess, of a world that overcomes (the covenantal) God. That it conceives a new God, maybe even one of transcendence, is not the ultimate issue, for such conception is conditioned by an intensification of immanence, of the world over against the given (covenantal) signification—which is to say of namelessness's excess to the improper naming of the divine. What apocalyptic affirms, above all, is the necessity of maintaining fidelity to the immeasurable, not as something positively named but as something that is there, that is real, such that its contravention by signification renders such signification inadequate.[18] Apocalyptic, according to this interpretation, is the affirmation of what is immeasurable over against the measure of signification (in this case, of covenantal signification). This means that apocalyptic may be used, in virtue of the same principle, as a means of evaluating any novel signification that it subsequently generates. An adequate concept of apocalyptic is thus one that allows apocalyptic to problematize not only what it replaces, but also what it engenders; it is, at base, an affirmation of an immeasurability that exceeds even that which is codified as apocalyptic.

It is along the lines of this conception of the apocalyptic that it becomes possible to resist the identification of apocalyptic with transcendence. If there is irruption in apocalyptic, then it is nothing more and nothing less than the irruption of what is already there, of an immanent namelessness. While it is necessary to signify the break thus occasioned, it is not necessary—it is in fact mistaken—to signify this break according to the lineaments of the transcendent. This is because such a move obscures the nature of the process by which apocalyptic emerges; the immeasurability of apocalyptic emergence is subsumed by the signification of the transcendent. It is, in fact, precisely such a subsumption that is involved in the logic of rupture, which accounts for the shift from preapocalyptic to apocalyptic signification in terms of the action of an eminent being. What I am suggesting, on the contrary, is an explanation of apocalyptic exteriority that proceeds through an immanent excess. The logic of transcendent irruption is thus rejected in favor of a discontinuity of immanence with itself. For a logic of discontinuity, what takes place in apocalyptic is not the arrival of something positive from beyond; it is rather the breakdown of the world as it is presently determined—that is,

18. For a more detailed account of the concept of the immeasurable, see Barber and Smith, "Too Poor for Measure," 1–15.

the breakdown of the measure of the world by the immeasurability of the world, the emergence of an immanent instability.

Returning, then, to the specific relation between Christianity and apocalyptic, it should be said that to assert, as some do, the necessity of thinking a distinctively "Christian" apocalyptic is to evade the determination of this relation. It is true that Christian logic is essentially apocalyptic, but what exactly was at stake in the logic that, now falling under the category of apocalyptic, was prominent in the context that pre-dated and eventually provided the milieu of Jesus's preaching? To adhere to Christian declaration is to believe in the divine kingdom's emergence, but the question remains: What, exactly, is the meaning? At stake here is not just whether Christian declaration is apocalyptic; it is more fundamentally what is meant by apocalyptic. The key difference, then, is the one between the logic of discontinuity and the logic of rupture. According to the former, Christian declaration should be seen, apocalyptically, as a signification of the world's discontinuity with itself, of the priority of immeasurability over every established form of measure. The advantage of discontinuity is that it articulates apocalyptic excess just as much as rupture does, but in doing so it also refuses the conflation of apocalyptic with a form of identity. Its decomposition of identities, or forms of signification, leads directly into the construction of a genuinely open future.

If depoliticization of Christian declaration occurs through the installation of a transcendent ontology, then apocalyptic, insofar as it is understood in terms of an immanent discontinuity, allows us to affirm Christian declaration's basically political character—its antagonism with the world as it is already established. Here politics means not the ontological alignment with a God that will rupture the world from outside, but instead the divine signification of the world's immeasurability. The kingdom of God declared by Jesus is a politics of radical upheaval; it names the liberation from dominative structures and the construction of new, differential solidarities, precisely because it is apocalyptic—precisely, that is, because it proceeds in virtue of the world's immeasurability with regard to what oppresses. The God whose kingdom is declared by Jesus is a God that converges with the immeasurability of the world. Schwartz contends that apocalyptic cannot be founded politically. He admits that "the *historical* apocalypses *are* often reactions to foreign domination (and sometimes to inadequate native rule)," but maintains nonetheless that when it comes to appreciating the apocalyptic mythology as such, it is not "reasonable to suppose that its 'emergence' and spread were mainly reactions to specific events of political history."[19] What Schwartz's argument fails to address, however, is the link between the ontological and political registers of apocalyptic. Thus, while it may be granted that apocalyptic is not reducible to an explicitly political response to an historical event, doing so does not entail an apolitical interpretation of apocalyptic. This is because apocalyptic, even when grasped through an ideological problematic, is immediately a signification of immanent excess. Apocalyptic is a counter-ideology, but it is such insofar as it claims that reality exceeds the boundaries effectuated by the covenant ideology. The ideological— or as I would put it, the significative—here implies the ontological, and the ontological implies the political. This last implication may not be evident when a delimited notion of politics is foregrounded, such that some events are "political" whereas others are "cultural" or "religious." If, however, we understand politics more broadly as the making of reality, then nothing could be more political than the claim that reality exceeds its signification, that it exceeds even the (covenantal) mode of relation that God has established with God's people.[20] It is thus evident, when the above understanding of apocalyptic is given to Jesus's declaration that the kingdom of God has come, that this declaration is political. Christian declaration, precisely because it is apocalyptic, calls for the alternative construction of the world.[21]

19. Schwartz, *Imperialism and Jewish Society*, 76.

20. An example of this covenant-breaking may be found in the following chapter's discussion of Paul's relation to Moses.

21. It will be tempting, at this point, for some (especially from a Marxist orientation) to call for a secularization of this apocalyptic politics. (For an account of the various ways in which the relation between communism and apocalyptic, as it is found in the preaching and writing of Thomas Müntzer, has been criticized and appropriated by Marxist thought, see Alberto Toscano's *Fanaticism*, 43–97.) If apocalyptic signifies a politico-ontological potentiality, then is it not best to delink this potentiality from the figure of Jesus? While I do not wish to accede to this delinking, this is not because I would insist that apocalyptic is somehow the "property" of Christianity. I would claim, more exactly, that it is impossible (and thus undesirable) to sever the ontological from the significative—this, of course, is the argument that I advanced in chapter 1. Marxist thought is committed to universalism, and while the ontological implications of apocalyptic— i.e., the immeasurability of the world—are likewise universal in virtue of immanence's namelessness, it remains the case that this namelessness must be signified. It is possible for this namelessness to exceed properly "Christian" signification (I have argued for this possibility in the present chapter), and even for it to exceed apocalyptic signification. By dint of the same logic, however, it is possible for such namelessness to exceed the secular

It is with regard to this emphasis on the potentiality of such construction that the separation of a discontinuous from a ruptural account of apocalyptic comes to the fore. The novelty of apocalyptic has nothing to do with an event whose being is simply other to the world, and everything to do with the constructability of the world's immeasure. Forms by which history is rendered continuous remain the object of irreducible antagonism, but such apocalyptic antagonism here occurs through a process of decomposing these forms and recomposing the worldly matter liberated from these forms. The futural dimension of apocalyptic thus resides in the decomposition and recomposition of the world—in the process of constructing differential forms—not in the transformation of the world from its present form to the form that ruptures. Apocalyptic breaks with the old aeon and calls forth a new aeon, but it does so by constantly making and remaking the new aeon—the new aeon is ever anew. Because apocalyptic is discontinuous rather than irruptive, it is not once for all, nor is it a unitary novum that is repeated many times; it is on the contrary a becoming-apocalyptic, without end. What is named by apocalyptic is the emergence of time in history—time that is not conditioned by, but inversely is the condition of, history. History is rendered discontinuous because there is time, and apocalyptic names the introduction of time, what Deleuze calls "the pure and empty form of time," into history.[22] Apocalyptic is not a direct theory of time, but it is the fictive signification of time's emergence in history. This is to say that there is no purely abstract apocalyptic, for it is always signified, but what is distinctively apocalyptic in such signification is the expression of a time that is irreducible to the historical boundaries normally effected by signification.

From Participation to Diaspora

One of the basic difficulties of a ruptural apocalyptic is the spatial imaginary upon which it relies: if there is an irruption of the divine into the world, an invasive action, then it becomes necessary to imagine two spaces, one of the world and another that lies outside the world (the divine space from which the irruption or invasion originates). The relevance of

signification. It is due to my commitment to *all* of these possibilities, then, that I remain suspicious of the desire to straightforwardly convert the politico-ontological potentiality of apocalyptic from Christian to (secular) Marxist signification.

22. Deleuze, *Difference and Repetition*, 135.

this difficulty becomes apparent as we turn from the matter of time to the matter of space, for such a turn presses upon us the task of understanding how one spatializes apocalyptic. How, in other words, does one inhabit space if one's inhabitation takes its cues from apocalyptic? And if one maintains a ruptural account of apocalyptic, then how can one inhabit the world while orienting oneself around something that comes from a space beyond the world? It is with regard to the force exerted by such questions that one constantly encounters in Christianity the theme of participation. While this theme is often associated with thinkers of the *analogia entis*, it would be mistaken to assume that participation is necessitated primarily by an analogical theory of being. After all, even Barth, the most prominent modern critic of this theory, proffered in its place the analogy of faith. The dispute concerned the determination of analogy but it presumed that some sort of analogy must be maintained, and this, I would contend, is because analogy is the only sustainable means of articulating the manner in which one distinct space participates in another distinct space. If apocalyptic is to be conceived in terms of rupture, then the only way of maintaining a relation between the subject and object of rupture, i.e., between the transcendent deity and the world, is through participation, such that what is ruptured gains redemption by participating in that which comes from beyond. Participation is fortuitously fitted for rupture because it admits a distinction between spaces—as rupture demands— while maintaining a connection between what has been distinguished—a connection without which rupture would become purely meaningless.

Yet if participation thus solves the peculiar challenge of connecting two distinguished spaces, another challenge remains, and this is to conceive how the logic of participation impacts the inhabitation of space in this world. Specifically, the impact is that the world becomes imagined, and thus inhabited, in a centripetal manner. When world-space is imagined in relation to divine-space, the former gains value only insofar as it is related to the latter, and this means that the point of relation—the place or territory where one participates—gains centrality. Within a logic of participation, then, there is necessarily a central territory that, even as it gains its value from its relation to the transcendent, becomes hegemonic over peripheral territories. The territory beyond requires a territory below that would centripetally gather participants into the transcendent territory. The effect of this logic is that the transcendence–rupture–participation conceptual constellation spatializes this world hierarchically. This may not be immediately evident, insofar as participation seems to relativize the entirety of the world-space before an irruptive transcendence, but it does become evident once we take seriously the need for participation in what ruptures: no territory has value in itself, for absolute value resides in the transcendent, but the territory that participates in the transcendent has greater value than those that do not participate.[23] Furthermore, it must be noted that the participational territory's "greater" value is not relative to the non-participational territory; it is "greater" because of its nearness to something that is absolutely other to both itself (the participational territory) and to the non-participational territory. This means that a primarily horizontal relation—i.e., a mutually constitutive relation—between territories is foreclosed in principle, for the participational territory understands itself in relation to what transcends it, rather than to what differs from it in the world-space. Participation thus spatializes the world according to an inside/outside binary that cannot avoid valorizing gathering over dispersal. What I am proposing, against participation and in favor of the concept of diaspora, is that there is only one, immanently expressed space, with no outside transcending it. If ruptural apocalyptic sets forth a participational account of spatialization, then discontinuous apocalyptic sets forth a diasporic account of spatialization. The apocalyptic discontinuity of time with historical forms demands expression in this world, and diaspora conceives the logic of this expression by immanently spatializing the world's immeasurability as the interstitial excess of territorial limits.

Before proceeding to further elaborate the concept of diaspora, however, I want to recall attention to the function I believe this concept can serve. I began this chapter with a consideration of the strange fact that is often encountered with regard to Christianity: that which is declared by Christianity may be easily counterposed by the historical performance of Christianity. While some see in this counterposition an indictment of Christianity as such, others find in it the demand to turn an ideal version

23. It might be asked whether it is possible for more than one territory to participate in the transcendent, such that one should speak of participational territor*ies*. My concern here, however, is to emphasize the formal character of participation, and so while it is quite possible that many territories participate in the transcendent, the differences between these territories are nullified in virtue of their participation. In other words, what ultimately matters is not the particularity of the territory that participates, it is rather the fact *that* it participates. It is in virtue of this latter characteristic that participational territories, at least at the formal level, count as one, and it is for this reason that I speak of a unitary participational territory.

of Christianity against its corruption. I claimed, on the contrary, that both of these attitudes fall short insofar as they leave unasked the question of how Christianity is able to find itself in this counterposition. What is of interest, in other words, is neither the condemnation nor the reclamation of Christianity; it is rather the possibility of thinking Christianity apart from this binary between ideal and actuality. The reason I have posed a focused critique of invariant forms, ruptural logic, and participational territories is that these supply the conceptual structure that enables this binarization between a true version of Christianity and an actual performance of this truth. In each of these conceptual instances, what Christianity proclaims is provided with a realized existence that is ultimately unaffected by the manner in which it is performed. The performance, of course, also seeks to realize this existence, but its effort to do so is never a matter of constructing the realization; it is instead a matter of reduplicating, in or through the space of the world, what has already been realized at the level of transcendence. It is a matter—to put it rather clumsily—of realizing the realization. Christianity, precisely because of its peculiar status as something that is both already realized and in need of realization, is able to withstand counterposition. In fact, to call attention to this counterposition is, in a sense, to consent to the essential logic of something that shuttles between otherwordly and thisworldly realizations. What I am calling for, as I advance the concepts of problematic (or differential) forms, discontinuous logic, and diasporic spatialization, is an account of Christianity that would not be capable of entering into—much less consenting to—counterposition, and thus that would not need to enter into the dialectics of condemnation and reclamation.

The possibility of such a Christianity is perhaps most evident as we turn to the concept of diaspora, for it is here that we address most explicitly the "afterlife" of Christian declaration. This is to observe that modes of opposing ideal and actual Christianity tend to rely on a severance of the teachings of Jesus from the tradition that, claiming fidelity to such teachings, proceeded (usually unsuccessfully) in his wake. If a counterpositional Christianity is to be avoided, then it will be important to find a new way to conceive a link between the teachings of Jesus, or Christian declaration, and the viability of a tradition that inherits this declaration—and it is precisely such a link, I will argue in what follows, that diaspora provides. Let me make clear, however, that this is not to *defend* the historical performance of those who claimed such inheritance; it is more precisely to conceive the

real possibility of performing this declaration, or of inheriting this tradition, in a novel (and superior) manner. Perhaps the greatest objection to
desiring a tradition that would seek to perform or affirmatively inherit this
declaration is that such performative inheritance ends up either coloniz-
ing the world or devaluing the world (or both). I assent to this objection;
I also refuse (as should be evident) any attempt to evade this objection by
claiming that "true" Christianity never called for such performance. What
I want to supply, most explicitly with the concept of diaspora, is something else, namely an account of a Christian tradition that could exist only
against such colonization and devaluation of the world. Note, however,
that this is not to say that "true" Christianity would never promote such
evils—in fact, it has. My concern therefore is not to address the question of
whether Christianity's historical performance was a proper representation
of true Christianity; it is to address the question of what we are to do with
Christianity, with our unavoidable inheritance of its tradition.[24]

Interparticularity and the Spatialization of Discontinuity

I have argued that the content of Christian declaration, far from requiring
its own identitarian form, calls for an alternatively characterized form, an
intrinsically differential form. Translated into terms of space, the rejection of identitarian forms means the repudiation of invariant territories,
while the construction of differential forms means the composition of
deterritorialized relations. Deterritorializaton, in other words, is directly
demanded by Christian declaration, such that this declaration's content
does not exist in an integrated manner prior to, or at some point after,

24. This seems, I admit, a rather strong claim insofar as it would imply that it is impossible to remain outside, and thus to be against, Christianity. Am I not advancing yet
another, if perhaps subtler, mode of Christian imperialism? I certainly hope this is not
the case. When I speak of an unavoidable inheritance I am not asserting that it is impossible to be against Christianity. More precisely, I am observing that even to be against
Christianity is to inherit it—indeed, I hope that those who seek to be against Christianity
would find in my account an ally, at least insofar as I am attempting to find a way outside
of the Christianity that one would wish to be against, and insofar as my account might
help provide a non-resentful relation to this inheritance. What I am trying to register and
think through, quite simply, is the fact that the discursive regimes invented by Christianity
have been rather pervasively installed. The nature of this invention and installation, along
with a more sustained attempt to think the implication of post-Christian discourse in the
inheritance of Christianity—in other words, what I have in mind when I speak, as I have
just done, of an "unavoidable inheritance"—will be addressed at length in chapter 4.

deterritorialization's process of decomposition and recomposition.[25] It is therefore mistaken to suppose that adherence to Christian declaration implies adherence to a Christian (or Christianized) territory, or that the integrity of a Christian discursive tradition requires repudiation of any contamination by what lies outside of it.[26] While this would seem to be the case with a logic of participation, it not at all the case with a diasporic logic, for which integrity and discontinuity—understood spatially as deterritorialization—are in a reciprocal rather than mutually exclusive relation.

In order to develop such a concept of diaspora, we can turn to some remarks made by John Howard Yoder in his essay, "On Not Being Ashamed of the Gospel." Yoder here addresses a tension that inevitably arises in the communication, or cultural translation, of Christian declaration. On one hand, the demand for communication calls for significative flexibility, understood as vulnerability to networks of signification that are foreign to those expressive of Christian declaration; on the other, the demand for integrity requires attention to ways in which such cultural translation might blunt the specific directives of Christian declaration. The tension, put in other terms, is one between universality (communicative flexibility) and particularity (communicative integrity).

Yoder expresses suspicion of what he calls "the standard epistemological context of establishment."[27] This is to say that the desire to make certain statements viable by subjecting them to pre-established, purportedly universal criteria is one that ought to be opposed. What is flawed is not the desire to communicate statements beyond their culturally embedded context; it is more precisely the desire to gain from such universal criteria a validity that is supposed to be otherwise lacking from particular statements. Concomitantly, the object of opposition is the epistemological dominance

25. Deterritorialization, it should be noted, is a central concept in the work of Deleuze and Guattari, and it is treated most extensively in their text, *A Thousand Plateaus*.

26. My understanding of "discursive tradition" is informed by Saba Mahmood's discussion of this concept in her *Politics of Piety*—a discussion, it should be noted, that is itself framed by Talal Asad's *Idea of an Anthropology of Islam*. Discursive tradition, Mahmood remarks, can "be understood along the lines of what Foucault calls a 'discursive formation,' a field of statements and practices whose structure of possibility is neither the individual, nor a collective body of overseers, but a form of relation between the past and present predicated on a system of rules that demarcate both the limits and the possibility of what is sayable, doable, and recognizable as a comprehensible event in all its manifest forms" (114–15).

27. Yoder, "On Not Being Ashamed of the Gospel," 45.

of invariant and universally encompassing criteria. Outside the bounds of this essay, Yoder has described more clearly the sort of "establishment" that he wants to resist: "Medieval European imperial Christendom, or Imperial Russian Orthodoxy, or the Enlightenment claims of the French encyclopedists, or the arbitrage today of the news media, or the professional historians, or university academics, have all claimed and can consistently claim that the place where they stand is in some sense more reasonable, more universal, than other places." The community set forth by Christian declaration, Yoder continues, "renounces such claims in principle."[28] What is thus opposed is a logic of universalism or establishment that, while found in various incarnations (and Yoder's examples are indicative rather than exhaustive), can be abstracted from these exemplars—hence it is opposed "in principle." This is not a protest against some specific misuse or immoderate exaggeration of universality. It is more fundamentally a protest against the mechanism of universality, its sheer principle, and the heart of this protest is that any act of universal establishment is involved in a kind of self-concealing violence. Something that is very much particular and contingent conceals this fact from itself in order to present itself as ahistorically valid, as intrinsically normative.[29]

We are now able to give more precision to Yoder's navigation of the tension between communication and integrity: difficulty arises not in the act of communication, but in the conditioning of this act by pre-established criteria. What therefore must be sought is a symbiotic relation between the particularity of Christian discourse, understood as that which takes the signification of Christian declaration as a distinctive mark of its own integrity, and the communication of Christian declaration beyond the bounds of Christian discourse. It may be noted that this leaves Christian discourse in a complex position: it is turned toward Christian declaration as the source of its own integrity, yet it is likewise turned toward that which lies outside the domain of Christian discourse, for such turning-outwards is what this declaration demands. Of course, this seems paradoxical only if one assumes that what is to be communicated is Christian discourse rather than Christian declaration, thereby forgetting that Christian discourse is nothing in itself. Whatever integrity Christian discourse has is gained from its adherence to the directions set forth by

28. Yoder, *Jewish-Christian Schism Revisited*, 114.

29. I advance this argument in my essay, "Epistemological Violence, Christianity, and the Secular," 271–93.

Christian declaration, and these directions necessarily lead outside of any sedimented Christian discourse. The principle of anti-establishment thus cuts both ways. It opposes not just the universal establishment to which the particularity of Christian discourse might be subjected, but also the particular establishment of Christian discourse. To oppose the universal establishment in the name of the particular establishment is to fail to be anti-establishment. Accordingly, what the principle of anti-establishment seeks to defend is not the particularity that, having already achieved its integrity, stands against the universal, but rather the relationship *between* particularities. What it promotes is neither the universal conditioning of the particular nor the particular exception to the universal, but rather the relation between particulars—what might be called the interparticular. This, I would contend, is where Yoder's remarks lead us, for only in this way can one stand against universal establishment (and thus for particularity) while also standing against particular establishment (and thus affirm interparticular communication). There is to be no opposition between particularity and communicability because communication is not subject to the universal, and because particularity is not integral in itself (for it can be Christian discourse only insofar as it undermines its apparent integrity by entering into the communication of Christian declaration).

To conceive this interparticular communication is to conceive diaspora. With diaspora there is no integrated discourse to be served; integrity resides not prior to but within diasporic disintegration (or within the differential forms produced in diaspora). In terms of cultural history—and a cultural approach is clearly central when we are addressing questions of translation—diaspora refers initially, of course, to Jewish identity. Therefore it is not accidental that Yoder, in thinking through the symbiotic relation of particular integrity and interparticular communication, first turns to Jewish history. The importance of this reference licenses an extensive quotation:

> The "ghetto" in European experience was not a place into which Jews chose to retreat, in order to be safe or to be kosher, or because gentiles could not understand them. The ghetto-dwellers did have a language of their own—two of them, in fact, one to read their scriptures and one for their family life—but they also spoke the Italian, the German, or the Polish of the city around them. They spoke it well enough to do business and to represent a cultural challenge. By the third generation in a new host setting they spoke the gentiles'

language well enough to serve the host culture as scribes, doctors, and traders, even though they still lived in the ghetto.[30]

What should become clear here is that diaspora is not a defensive accommodation of particularity to universal establishment; it is not a fall from some ideal purity of particular existence. Diaspora is affirmative, and it is affirmative not of particularity's integrity over against universality, but rather of the freedom of particularity to be interparticular—that is, to treat supposed establishments as nothing more nor less than additional particulars, and to understand its own particularity as integrally translational. In fact, on Yoder's account the defensive reaction belongs to the establishment, which defines itself precisely through its fear of diaspora's free use of particularity. "It was the gentile establishment, not Jewry, who walled off the ghetto, to defend itself against the cultural threat of the Jews' dissonant, often more energetic and more creative life style."[31] Diaspora exercises a creative capacity that is lacking in the universal establishment, and it is perhaps in order to stymie this capacity that the universal establishment wants to see Jewish existence as a particular establishment, when in fact it is interparticularly opposed to establishment of any kind. Note, furthermore, that there is no question, for Jewish existence, of an a priori contradiction between particular integrity and interparticular communication (though of course this does not mean there are no challenges of pragmatic negotiation), even as this interparticular communication comes to construct the very character of Jewish existence. Diaspora does not merely hold together, as if it were conducting a balancing act, the imperatives of particular integrity and communicative deterritorialization. More precisely, diaspora proceeds by imagining a positive, mutually constitutive relation between these two imperatives and thus accedes to a process of interparticular decomposition and recomposition.

Returning to Christian discourse, it can be said that diaspora emerges in the tension between territories—the territory already constructed through the composition of differential forms and the territory that is encountered as other (what Yoder calls the "host culture"). The Christian territory, if indeed it is one that emerges through adherence to the content of Christian declaration, is one that already harbors the dissonant—after all, the forms constructed by Christian declaration are meant to be differential

30. Yoder, "On Not Being Ashamed of the Gospel," 48–49.
31. Ibid., 49.

rather than identitarian. But even such a territory comes up short insofar as it is taken in itself: though the forms it has composed are differential, the assemblage of these forms will fall back into a collective identitarianism apart from additional encounter with an other. Deterritorialization is both object and subject of Christian declaration, precisely because it refuses to grant priority to the subjectivity of Christian discourse or to the objectivity of the host culture, both of which have a tendency to sediment into auto-referential—which is to say transcendent—territories. In this respect, deterritorialization is immanent discontinuity, or the mutual immanence of discontinuous territories; it involves the active problematization, by the proper namelessness of immanence, of the signification generated by territorial cultures. Such signification is not to be negated, but its improper creativity will be unleashed only insofar as its tendency to auto-referentially set itself up as proper is decomposed.

The deterritorializing character of Christian declaration thus requires a process in which the real tension between Christian discourse— understood as the territorial composition engendered by Christian declaration—and the discourse of the host culture is affirmed. For the declaration to truly be good news, it must be able to offer something that is not already given in the established signification of the host culture. "The reasons which count to move hearers to accept the 'news' as 'good' cannot already be provided by 'public and shared criteria' already present in every culture, for then no news would be needed, or possible."[32] In this sense, the particularity of Christian signification is not something to be conditioned by the established signification of the host culture. At the same time, in order for this encounter to be a truly deterritorializing one, the otherness must go in both directions. The otherness of the host culture's signification is just as important as the otherness of what is declared apart from this host culture. Only in this way does Christian signification evade the lure of transcendent auto-referentiality; only in this way does it make particularity into a means of becoming interparticular. "That news should be accredited as 'good' by a receptor culture requires first that it be present there, in forms which make sense there."[33] The demand to become sensible to a network of signification that is other to what has already been composed in Christian signification is what introduces the tension necessary for deterritorialization. In fact, Yoder goes so far as to call this

32. Ibid., 50.
33. Ibid., 49.

an act of *submission*: "The 'reasons which count' are present in the intra-subjective communication setting, by virtue of the fact that the newsbearers have entered the scene, submitting to the language of the host culture, articulating and incarnating their values in the neighbors' terms."[34] It is in this deterritorializing tension, where both sides of territorial otherness are valorized, that the centrality of discontinuity to Christian declaration, the centrality of differentiality to integrity, is pursued.

The differential forms composed by signification of Christian declaration become impotent if they are not subjected to the further differential encounter with the otherness of the host culture. There is no doubt that the differentiality of Christian declaration may decompose sedimented forms of the host culture, but such differentiality must also decompose the already composed differential forms of Christian signification. The consequence of this is that what is communicated in the signification of Christian declaration changes—and not just accidentally—in the process of deterritorializing communication. Let us recall that the difference invoked by Christian declaration stems not from the possession of a special Christian form in opposition to other forms, but rather from the insistence that form must become differential rather than identitarian (a difference of formal character, rather than of formal content). There is no invariance to the differential forms composed in virtue of Christian declaration, so how can it be the case that what is communicated would stay the same throughout the process of its communication?

Diaspora is therefore not the means by which Christian declaration passes into and through the world—if it were, then it would amount to an alibi for participation—it is rather the intrinsic expression of this declaration; the discontinuity articulated by diaspora is not entered into from a position in which Christian declaration first possesses itself, for Christian declaration is always already discontinuous. It is in this sense that Nathan Kerr's recent account of Christian diaspora, which depends on the concept of "dispossession," runs into difficulty.[35] There can be no dispossession, for there is no initial possession. Kerr sees the aim of this dispossessive dynamic as the "*transformation* of the historically contingent as such."[36]

34. Ibid., 50.

35. See Kerr, *Christ, History and Apocalyptic*, 179, 187–88, 194–95.

36. Ibid., 131. It is not coincidental, in view of my argument for a link between the logic of participation (of which I take Kerr's transformational approach to be an instance) and the logic of rupture, that Kerr is a proponent of Martyn's account of "invasive action."

Manifest dispossession becomes the handmaiden of a latent commitment to the idea that one already has in hand the cipher according to which the world is to be transformed. One is, of course, dispossessed of this cipher, but only in order to more adequately transform the world that dispossesses into the form of which one is dispossessed. Yet the world, on my account of diaspora, is not something to be transformed, it is something that is to be differentially composed. Such composition proceeds not according to the outlines of an invariant form, which would transform the "historically contingent" into that which participates in a substantive Christ, but instead according to a deterritorializing movement that is without end. There is nothing lacking in the historically contingent as such; it is not in need of transformation—if anything, the liberation called for by Christian declaration involves the freedom to be more contingent, or the liberation from the purportedly necessary forms that are decomposed by the differential dynamism of diaspora. What matters, then, is not transformation but deformation, not historical contingency's sublation but its liberation. It is, after all, the sheer contingency of the world, its anarchic potentiality in excess of invariant forms of identity, which enables the composition of differential forms. The power of the diasporic movement set forth by Christian declaration thus lies not in the gathering of this surplus of contingency into a superior form of Christ, but instead in the promotion of the discontinuity engendered by the signification of this surplus.

It is such promotion of discontinuity that is aimed at in Yoder's injunction that any signification of Christian declaration must submit to the signification of the host culture. This is, once again, not a mediating strategy for successfully winning the host culture to the side of Christian declaration. It is, on the contrary, a novel repetition of Christian declaration that becomes good news only insofar as it is deterritorialized by the encounter with signification that remains other. This, in fact, is the very reason for the emphasis on "submission": only in this way is a genuine encounter able to occur, only in this way is the tendency to latch onto one's purported identity undone. Interparticularity requires the ability to decompose, to render discontinuous, the identifying form of one's particularity. Along these lines, Yoder remarks that Christian declaration,

---

Kerr sees apocalyptic logic as one that "stresses a God who is utterly different from this world, who breaks into this world from beyond," one that "thus names the particular operation of God's *transcendence*, conceived according to the prior inbreaking of God's Kingdom into history from beyond" (12–13).

if it is to be good news, "cannot be imposed by authority, or coercively. It is rendered null when assent is imposed"—and this, I would add, is because it exists only in the discontinuity that is nullified by imposition.[37] The imposition of Christian signification on the signification of the host culture is not a failed application of Christian declaration; it is the refusal to make this declaration, for it is the refusal to affirm discontinuity. Christian declaration decomposes the already given forms of identity that govern signification, but it is able to compose differential forms only insofar as it submits to the surplus of signification unleashed, within the host culture, by the liberation of historical contingency from the presumptive forms of necessity that are decomposed. The deterritorializing encounters of diaspora thus free space from transcendent signification—by opening a discontinuous space in between territories—in order to immanently construct the improper surplus of immanence.

---

37. Yoder, "On Not Being Ashamed of the Gospel," 50.

3

The World in the Wake
of Pauline Thought

The point in Paul is that even in perfection I am not an I, but we are a we.

I can imagine as an apocalyptic: let it go down.
I have no spiritual investment in the world as it is.

—Jacob Taubes[1]

Pauline Thought as Theopolitical Antagonism

THE DIASPORIC CONCEPTION OF Christianity with which I concluded the previous chapter is one, to be sure, that has not been determinative in the formation of our understanding of Christianity. This is perhaps most notable when we consider the nature of Christian identity, or the identification of something that comes to be called Christianity. What I would like to pursue in the present chapter is an account of Pauline thought that attends to the way in which such thought addressed the complex passage from Christian declaration to Christian identity. If a problematic or differential understanding of Christianity does not emerge in the aftermath of Pauline thought, then why is this the case?[2] We can gain

1. Taubes, *Political Theology of Paul*, 56, 103.
2. I should make clear that I am not here attempting to demonize Paul while sanctifying

the outlines of a response to this question, I believe, by foregrounding the question of community. While it is certainly the case that the problem of community is already there in Jesus, the pressure that this problem can exert becomes manifest with Paul, who takes Christian declaration in new directions. In a basic sense, this movement in new directions is implicit in Christian declaration, which calls for the undoing of identities and the composition of differential forms. Must not this undoing issue in a going forth, a deterritorializing, diasporic movement? This is certainly the message that Paul discerns, and it is in this register that the question of community arises. Community, however, cannot be founded on an identity that is already present, for such an identity is precisely what is challenged by Christian declaration. How then is community to be thought? This question becomes especially pressing when it comes to the community of Jews and Greeks, or more exactly of Jewish *Christians* and Greek *Christians*. At stake is the very idea of what it would mean to be, or to become, "Christian." What sort of thing is Christianity? What kind of status should be granted to this third term between "Jew" and "Greek"? At the heart of Pauline thought is an attempt to affirm not only the deterritorialization effected by Christian declaration, but also the possibility of a community that would be composed through, and in the wake of, this diasporic movement.[3] Pauline thought thus belongs to the paradoxical need to establish a discourse on that which undermines discourse, to conceive a commonality of that which undermines identity, and to imagine the connectivity running though a discontinuous diaspora. Given the difficult tensions intrinsic to such paradoxes, it will be unsurprising if Paul's resolutions remain unsatisfying. What is necessary, however, is not just a

---

Jesus. My aim, in other words, is not somehow to claim that Jesus "got Christianity right" whereas Paul corrupted it. There is, once again, no essence of Christianity to "get right." My aim, on the contrary, is to understand what it was about Christian declaration that enabled it to become understood transcendently rather than immanently, or as identitarian rather than diasporic. As will hopefully be made clear in what follows, Pauline thought is not a contravention of something that was already self-consciously diasporic so much as an ambivalent, internally conflictual attempt—and one, I will contend, that is ultimately unsatisfying—to think consistently an inchoate problematic.

3. Of course, we must be careful not to impute to Paul a concept of Christianity that, though available to us, was certainly not available to him (even if this concept of Christianity was made possible by his efforts). We are, in other words, addressing the invention of Christianity, which is to say the passage from Christian declaration to a community engendered by this declaration.

critique of Paul, but also a reclamation of the problem to which he sought to become adequate.

My account, in what follows, depends on the work of Jacob Taubes—primarily certain arguments advanced in his late text, *The Political Theology of Paul* (which tends mostly to "Romans"), though some reference will also be made to his very early survey of apocalyptic thought, *Occidental Eschatology*. What is intriguing about Taubes is his ability to contextualize Paul not just apocalyptically, but also politically. It is in fact the very link between the apocalyptic and the political that shapes his understanding of Paul. While there are surely other dynamics at work, my selection of this dynamic, as it is foregrounded by Taubes, is driven by its ability to address the relation between discontinuity (conceived by Taubes under the theme of apocalyptic) and community. Such a relation is at the heart of the establishment of something called "Christianity," an establishment that, insofar as it concerns the making of the world, of possibilities of existence, is always already political. Taubes is able to inject this political decision on the possibilities of existence back into Pauline thought. It is thus with Taubes's interpretation that we may begin to examine the relation between Pauline thought—so central to the invention of Christianity, to the establishment of what will come to be an invariant Christian discourse—and the logic of differential composition that I have claimed is intrinsic to Christian declaration, and that I want to conceive as the heart of diaspora.

Turning now to Taubes's understanding of Paul, we must observe straightaway the interpretation he gives to Paul's concept of "law." This term is frequently taken as the identifying mark of Jewish existence. Accordingly, to speak of "law" is to speak of the complex dynamic at work in the establishment of a Christian body that is Jewish as well as Gentile. If such a body is to be established, then the primacy of law must be undermined, for the primacy of law means the primacy of Jewish existence, and it is precisely this last primacy that must give way to an equality, in Christ, between Jews and Gentiles. Of course, a certain primacy of the law, and of Jewish existence, *is* maintained, insofar as it is through God's historical relationship to the Jews that the messianic aeon of Christ emerges, but the point of this primacy is to give way to the messianic arrival. In this sense, the primacy of Jewish existence is relativized by the very emergence that it conditions, namely the new age of Christ in which the old division between Jew and Gentile no longer holds sway. A great deal of important work has been done over the past several decades to show that the fundamental interest of the dialectic of law and grace in "Romans" is not the justification of the individual believer but rather the constitution of a people that is both Jew and Gentile, a people in which this division is undone by the new covenant established by the faith of Christ.[4]

Recognition of the fact that Paul's concern is not the individual but the community is manifest in Taubes's work. He notes that the congregation in Rome is not unlike the congregation in Galatia, which receives from Paul the letter that most aggressively attacks those who would make circumcision, a distinctive mark of Jewish existence, into the condition of Christian existence. Those whom Paul opposes "come along and say: It's all well and good that you have your Christ, but without circumcision there can't be anything to it. I'm not even going to sit at one table with you!"[5] What is at stake is not individual justification but the mundane, pragmatic problem of a common body. "The whole question of commensality, of the common table, these are very concrete problems. Does one eat together? Does one sleep together? Is this a congregation or is this not a congregation?"[6] The concept of law, whether in the context of the Galatians or the Romans, concerns the composition of a congregation or community that would move, differentially, beyond the formal opposition of Jewish identity and Gentile identity. So, for Taubes, there is no question of an individualizing locus of the law; law is always about community—but is law *only* about community? What Taubes grasps is that law invokes not just the question of community, but also the question of politics. Law is the *link* between the communal and the political, for the politics of Christian declaration is turned not only within, toward the commonality of Jew and Gentile, but also without, toward the political sovereignty of Rome.

The fact that Paul's understanding of Christianity is immediately politicized can be seen, Taubes claims, by the introductory lines of "Romans." In this opening Paul describes himself as one "called to proclaim the

4. Harink, *Paul Among the Postliberals*, 15–16, helpfully summarizes this "New Perspective" as one marked by the "shifting [of] attention from the typically 'Lutheran' or Protestant themes of individual justification, sin, guilt, grace and faith to the more concrete, historical issues of the relationships between Jews and Gentiles in Paul's mission and churches. Justification, for example, is about how it is that Gentiles have come, through Jesus Christ, to share in the life of God's people, Israel."

5. Taubes, *Political Theology of Paul*, 21.

6. Ibid.

gospel of God, . . . the gospel concerning his Son, who was descended from David according to the flesh and was declared to be Son of God with power according to the spirit of holiness by resurrection from the dead."[7] There is an abundance of predication here, and, in the wake of the long duration of Christian hegemony, it may be difficult to feel the force of what Paul is asserting. "Son of God," Taubes notes, is an "ascribed" rather than "natural quality," it is significative—in other words, *political*—rather than ontological. And what does "Son of God" signify, or what takes place in this act of signification? The ascription of this quality to Jesus "is an act of enthronement," it is "a conscious emphasis of those attributes that are imperatorial, kingly, imperial."[8] In brief, then, Paul's introductory statement is a direct assault on the sovereignty of Roman imperial authority—this is already the case simply in virtue of the signification "Son of God," but it should additionally be observed that it is said to "the congregation in Rome, where the imperator is himself present, and where the center of the cult of the emperor, the emperor religion, is located."[9] The "good news," the Christian declaration, is that the emperor has been deposed, sovereignty has been broken, new possibilities of existence are now available.

These new possibilities are not private, they are not individual, but are instead public or political, declared all the way into Rome, into the essential territory of sovereignty. It is important, Taubes says, to keep in mind that Paul "could, after all, have introduced [his letter] pietistically, quietistically, neutrally, or however else; but there is none of that here."[10] To signify Jesus as the Son of God is to set forth a political antagonism that holds nothing in reserve; its claim that the world as it presently stands has come to an end is one that is universal in scope, and that brooks no compromise. In this sense, Paul refuses the gambit that will come to characterize the mainstream of Christian discourse, namely the separation of interior and exterior, such that Christ's rule can take place without fundamentally calling into question, or problematizing, the given political ordering of existence. Taubes elsewhere claims, in his historical account of eschatological thought, that the tipping point—the point at which the political theology of Paul is grafted onto an interior/exterior

7. Ibid., 14; Rom 1:1–4.

8. Taubes, *Political Theology of Paul*, 14.

9. Ibid.

10. Ibid., 16.

duality—can be found in Augustine, where the tendency to claim that the "destiny of the soul is central" prevails.[11] The alternative political process set forth by Christian declaration is grafted onto the individual soul, and thus leaves space for a non-apocalyptic politics. Yet even though this may come to be the case for Christianity it is certainly not the case for Paul, for whom political theology, and not the soul's destiny, is central. Such a political theology is irreducibly antagonistic towards the Powers that presently govern the world, so much so that "Romans," even as it concerns the making of a Christian (Jewish and Gentile) community, is also—and even moreso—concerned with the making of being itself. This letter is in essence "a *political* declaration of war on the Caesar."[12]

How, then, does one get from law, which belongs to the question of community, to a political antagonism with regard to Rome? One does not do this by imagining a situation in which, simply by being a community, one resists Rome—there is a deeper link, for the concept of law is always already political (and never merely communal). This, in any case, is what Taubes argues: "the critique of law is a critique of a dialogue that Paul is conducting not only with the Pharisees . . . but also with his Mediterranean environment."[13] The upshot of Taubes's contention is that Paul's concept of law—which is, of course, a concept of what he seeks to overcome—refers not just to a Torah-defined identity, something that would be an obstacle for Jewish-Gentile community, but more broadly to a determination of political (imperial) sovereignty, something that would be an obstacle for a politically antagonistic theology. The Pauline "concept of law . . . is a compromise formula for the Imperium Romanum."[14] Taubes paints a picture of an era in which significant religious or cultural differences were superseded by a common adherence to law. This law may have had different specific features according to particular religio-cultural differences, but what was universal was "law" as such—the situation was one of cosmopolitan unity-amidst-difference. This means that even though law could carry various valences, depending on the particular religio-cultural context at issue, specific differences were nullified at a general level. Disagreement at the level of particularity gave way to an overarching agreement that law—regardless of the particular flavor that it was

11. Taubes, *Occidental Eschatology*, 80.

12. Taubes, *Political Theology of Paul*, 16.

13. Ibid., 25.

14. Ibid., 23.

given—was universally regnant and ultimately one. Taubes claims that "there was an aura, a general Hellenistic aura, an apotheosis of nomos. One could sing it to a Gentile tune, this apotheosis—I mean, to a Greek-Hellenistic tune—one could sing it in Roman, and one could sing it in a Jewish way. Everyone understood law as they wanted to."[15] I would add that this last point is especially important, for law, despite its particular incarnations, was able to determine the limits of being, of what was possible, even amidst its malleability. Law named a form of forms, it named the character of formality, such that the specific differences between one version of law and another remained, at least in the last instance, accidental. Thus to stand against law, as Paul did, was not just to stand against Torah-defined identity; it was to stand against "Greek-Hellenistic" cosmic order and Roman power—it was, in short, to stand against a simultaneously flexible and delimiting liberalism, a multicultural context of resonance that, as *nomos*, spanned differences of specificity.[16] Accordingly, when Taubes poses the question of the meaning of "law," when he asks if Paul means "the Torah, . . . the law of the universe, . . . natural law," he is able to answer: "It's all of these in one. Everything is bound up with everything else. But that's not Paul's mistake, it's due to the aura."[17] In other words, the omnivalence of law is due not to a theoretical vagueness in Paul, but to the historical context—at once cultural, social, legal, philosophical, theological—that he inhabited, and opposed. Only when this is understood does it become possible to understand what Paul intends in his critical opposition to law.

If Pauline thought is, at bottom, a radically anti-Roman, anti-nomic political theology, it is so by way of discontinuity. That which happens with Jesus is not conditioned by Rome, by the law, and this is to the detriment of the law. Something has exceeded the form of Roman sovereignty. Taubes notes that Paul's thought is driven by a "protest" so absolute that it amounts to "a transvaluation of values: It isn't *nomos* but rather the one who was nailed to the cross by *nomos* who is the imperator!"[18] This is a fundamental reversal, for it entails a rejection of the Powers that govern existence, of the universality inherent to that which is said to exist. Paul's

---

15. Ibid.

16. The use of some of these terms is, of course, anachronistic—the point, however, is to foreground the way in which Paul's context could be said to resemble our own.

17. Taubes, *Political Theology of Paul*, 24.

18. Ibid.

thought is also universal, of course, but it is a universality of a different order. Paul's universality, Taubes says, "is nothing like nomos as *summum bonum*,"[19] which is to say that there is no attempt to synthesize, to bring everything together in perfection. On the contrary, the universality of Pauline political theology is one that is marked by its founding discontinuity; it seeks universality, but it begins with the particularity of Jesus. It is a universality that cannot seek to encompass all, for it commences with rejection—a double rejection, in fact, whereby the rejection of Jesus by the law demands a rejection of the law by the adherents of Christian declaration. Pauline universality thus starts with a decision, with partiality, and it is for this reason that it cannot coincide with the universality of the law; it begins with discontinuity and should, at least in principle, proceed in a similar manner.

At the base of Taubes's Paul, then, is a decision—one, it should be noted, that joins the theological to the political—and it is for this reason that a peculiar mutual appreciation can emerge between Taubes and Carl Schmitt. Of course, there is also a rather severe disagreement: the former wishes to unleash the forces of chaos, the anarchic—this is why apocalyptic, or discontinuity, is always good news for the poor—whereas the latter seeks to hold this apocalyptic force of discontinuity at bay, and all the more insofar as he recognizes the power with which it threatens law. The political-theological link, here, is found in the decision, which is itself groundless, and which may seek either to unleash or to control the differential movement that is articulated by an apocalyptic Jesus and spatialized by diaspora. In what direction does Paul decide?

On one hand, Paul calls for the liberation from law, and thus for the emergence of something like differential composition, which would be possible once the order of the present world is undone. It is this aspect that Yoder stresses in his account of what Paul calls the Powers—these are, Yoder says, analogous to what we call "structures." Powers, analogously understood through the concept of structure, "point to the patterns or regularities that transcend or precede or condition the individual phenomena we can immediately perceive"; the concept "points in all its modulations to some kind of capacity to make things happen."[20] While there is a positive function exercised by the Powers, insofar as they allow a degree

19. Ibid.
20. Yoder, *Politics of Jesus*, 138.

of ordered existence, they are ultimately oppressive. The Powers capture our attention and thus lead us to accept that the possibilities they signify coincide with the possibilities of existence.[21] Set against this backdrop, the discontinuity introduced by Jesus becomes a declaration that life is to be lived apart from these Powers, or a declaration by Taubes's Paul that the law has been surpassed. One sees here the emergence of an alternative signification, or more precisely of the capacity to produce polyglossial signification. Political theology, under the heading of discontinuity, calls for the differential composition of peoples, united synchronically in a transvaluation of values, such that there is no identitarian form of law governing immanent existence. Immanence, once again, is immanent to nothing but itself. The signification of Christian declaration, extending from Jesus to Paul, is an assertion of nameless immanence's discontinuity with the naming of the Powers. One could even say that what is signified is the discontinuity of world with the Powers that nomistically determine it, such that the former exceeds the latter. The signification of Christian declaration underdetermines the overdetermination of the Powers, thus liberating the signification of the world from the supposedly primordial name of the law.[22]

On the other hand, it is also the case that this distinction between the world and the Powers' determination of the world, as I have just imagined it, is not fully pursued in Paul's thought. The limitation of such a pursuit is engendered by the direct mapping of the political-theological antagonism between Roman imperial power (law) and Christ onto the opposition between world and Christ. Concomitantly, to be against Rome is to be against the world. When this takes place, it must be asked: Has the universality of Paul's political theology ultimately disengaged itself from the universality of law? There is, as I have already remarked, a notable difference insofar as Paul's universality is founded in a discontinuity, such that the value of Christ cannot be given sense within, but only against—as a radical *transvaluation* of—the value of law. Still, for a full departure from law to take place, it must be the case that the form of value, and not just the particular signification of value (law or Christ), is discontinuous.

21. For an account of the centrality of "attention" to questions of religion, see Goodchild, *Capitalism and Religion*.

22. I have presented an account of Yoder's theory of "the Powers" in terms of overdetermination in my essay, "Particularity of Jesus and the Time of the Kingdom," 63–89.

The particularity of Jesus, which is the condition for Pauline universality, is a worldly event, an immanent happening. It is not out of place, then, to suppose that this happening might proceed in a worldly manner, as an immanent re-composition of the world. Yet this possibility is overlooked insofar as the world is identified with the Powers—that is, insofar as the world, rather than the given determination of the world, is made into the political-theological enemy of Christ. When the world is identified with the Powers, the synchronic or a priori antagonism between Roman imperial power and Christ is preserved, but the diachronic composition of this antagonism is underplayed, if not lost. If anything of the diachronic antagonism does remain, it is only as it is filtered through the transcendent lens of this synchronic antagonism, such that worldly signification is less a re-composition of the world than a composition of Christ against the world. The immanence of the founding antagonism and the diachronic—or diasporic—composition of this antagonism is lost. This is to say that discontinuity persists at the level of foundation, but not at the level of composition, such that the demand for composition itself to be discontinuous, or differential, is abandoned. The particularity of Paul's political theology, founded as it is in Jesus, should—according to my immanent, diasporic account of Christianity—figure in not just as the founding instance of a new universality, but also as a different way of being universal, namely by being interparticular. The discontinuity of a particular Jesus with the universality of the Powers ought to give way to a compositional affirmation of the discontinuity between particular cultures of signification. It is in this regard that the Pauline contribution to the invention of Christianity—that is, of an identifiable culture of Christianity—should be problematized. Accordingly, even though the question of a communality of Jewish Christians and Gentile Christians must be seen in relation to Paul's political-theological antagonism towards cosmopolitan law, this political-theological antagonism must be linked back to the question of communality, for it is here, in the possibility of interparticular composition, that the apocalyptic politics of Christ must be diasporically constructed—it is here, in other words, that there might be a discontinuity not just of content but of form.

Taubes registers in his own way the challenge that emerges when discontinuity refers only to signifying content and not to form, when discontinuity of content is placed within an overarching continuity of form. Describing the historical progression of Christianity within and against

Rome, he writes: "The superego of Christ is seen by the masses as opposing Caesar. It outshines and devalues the Caesarian superego."[23] A difficulty thus emerges amidst the invention of Christianity, for the obstacle may very well arise not from the content of Caesar so much as from the form of "superego"—in other words, from the form of normative identity. How is this Christic norm different from the Caeserian norm? How, in other words, are we to express a Christian difference if the character of its form is not different? The resolution of this question regarding the nature of the difference is that the form of Christ comes from beyond, whereas the form of Caesar—or Rome, or law—comes from this world. This is indicated by Taubes: "the true god-king becomes a *protest* against this world, against the world of the empire and its emperor-saviors. Once the masses place all their hopes in a single man who is supposed to heal the sickness of the world, the dreams of man, who has thus given himself over, wander restlessly, and—since the fantasies of a 'political' savior remain unfulfilled—men finally end up in the belief in the 'true' savior from above."[24] The universal of the world is opposed in the name of the universal "from above," despite the fact that this latter universal is founded in particularity, and in the world. Political theology becomes less a way of being politically within the world (differential composition) and more a way of being politically against—because ontologically beyond—the world. Political theology becomes transcendent.

Four Points of Ambivalence in Pauline Thought

There is, I am arguing, an ambivalence at the heart of Paul's political-theological inflection of Christian declaration in terms of Christ's antagonism towards law. On one hand, discontinuity emerges as an immanent decomposition and recomposition of a world liberated from purportedly sovereign determination. On the other, discontinuity sediments into a stark opposition between the world (given over to the Powers) and the transcendent. This is primarily of interest not as an issue in Pauline scholarship, but as an exemplification of what is at stake in a logic of discontinuity. It is not even a matter of understanding Christianity as such, for this apocalyptic discontinuity that is in play in Christianity's emergence

23. Taubes, *Occidental Eschatology*, 65.
24. Ibid.

can be understood as the condition of possibility *for* Christianity, rather than a predicate of Christianity. If Christianity, and now Pauline thought, assumes a central role in this investigation, it is because, historically, Christianity becomes the carrier of discontinuity, the host of a viral discontinuity. To make discontinuity into the predicate of Christianity is to get things backwards, to make the affirmation of discontinuity—of apocalyptic and diasporic themes—dependent on the affirmation of an already established Christianity. What matters instead is the ability to address discontinuity in terms of a pre-history of Christianity, as a theoretical matrix that makes possible the invention of Christianity. Concomitantly, one can evaluate the potentialities and limitations effected by this invention in terms of discontinuity. From the vantage of a philosophy of immanence, discontinuity is irreducible, for immanence is nameless yet productive of excessive, fictive signification. A discontinuity will always obtain between being and its expression, and the affirmation of such discontinuity is vital in any effort to make the surplus of signification compose possibilities of existence that move beyond the given. This is what happens in Paul's political theology, which is able to break with the most fundamental determinations of being by breaking with the idea that the signification of law corresponds to reality. The life of Jesus, as interpreted by Paul, reveals that the signification of law is fictive—but how does one signify this falseness? Furthermore, what kind of signification does one generate in the wake of the breakdown of law?

It would be mistaken to assume that one can merely stand apart from the fray of signification, that one can articulate the philosophical lineaments of discontinuity but never examine and experiment with the significations of this discontinuity. This, it is worth re-stating, was one of the key lessons performed by Spinoza, who, even as he secularized being and opposed theological transcendence, still sought to selectively re-express certain religious themes, to direct a properly nameless immanence by means of fictive signification. One may engage similarly with Paul, in order both to examine how he signifies discontinuity and, in his wake, to begin to experiment with alternative manners of signification. It is a matter of praising the political antagonism and the articulation of discontinuity at work in Pauline thought while also tracing—and resisting—the limits that the invention of Christianity, still *in utero* with Paul, places on these very dynamics. This intersection, within signification, of discontinuity and limitation, can be indicated by a constellation of the concepts of people, love, chaos, and world.

People

Taubes claims that Paul, when he mentions the possibility of wishing himself "accursed and cut off from Christ for the sake of [his] own people, [his] kindred according to the flesh," is quite consciously comparing himself to Moses.[25] Paul's choice, Taubes adds, departs from Moses's choice, it chooses otherwise, but nonetheless Moses remains the standard. In short, this is not a question of suffering like—and thus imitating—Jesus; it is rather a question of imitating (even if by way of negation) Moses. What is at issue, for Paul, is whether he is going to cut himself off from Christ in order to remain with his "kindred according to the flesh," or whether he is going to remain bound to Christ and thus face the task of brining about a new people. Paul's concern, like Moses's concern, is "the *establishment and legitimation of a new people of God*."[26] If we are to speak of the invention of Christianity, then we must speak of a people, and this people is founded, at least explicitly, in Paul—hence Taubes is able to remark, "Christianity has its origin not properly in Jesus but in Paul."[27] Yet the analogy between Paul and Moses involves not just the common task of establishing a people, but also the sense that such establishment emerges or reveals itself ultimately in a moment of crisis. The constitution of a people is forced by the disequilibrium of God's relation to the people: in the case of Moses, it was a matter of having worshipped the golden calf; in the case of Paul, it was a matter of the rejection of God's messiah. According to Taubes it is an issue of "God's anger," which "wants to annihilate the people because it has sinned, because it has broken away."[28]

This is obviously true, but it seems there is a deeper logic that comes into sight once we contextualize God's anger within its larger network of relations. We should note, first of all, that divine anger is not a starting point so much as a catalyst. There is no destruction of a people, or no threat of destruction, without the invention—or preservation—of a people. Divine destruction is thus connected to popular liberation, to the production of novel modes of common existence. Furthermore, this

25. Rom 9:3.

26. Taubes, *Political Theology of Paul*, 28. Emphasis in original.

27. Ibid., 40.

28. Ibid., 28.

disequilibrium is not something that emerges only at the moment of sin and God's consequent anger. There is disequilibrium from the very beginning; it is always already there insofar as the constitution of a people emerges in relation to God, who is other to the people. The doublet of sin and divine anger is thus only a modality of a prior disequilibrium, a disequilibrium that makes possible the construction of something else. Divine anger and the threat to cut off the people thus point back to the impropriety of the initial covenant. They witness to the unnatural or fictive character of the relation that is being severed, and it is here that a certain redemption emerges: if a relation can be destroyed, this is because it has already been created, and if such a relation can be created, then it can also be re-created—or re-composed—after, or even through, destruction. We might understand forgiveness along these lines, namely as the re-creation, after having passed through destruction, of a relation between God and a people.

Taubes claims not only that Paul's thought belongs to the same kind of experience that Moses underwent, but also that this Mosaic experience—in which Moses pleads that God would forgive the people, that God would release the people (and Godself) from God's own oath to punish sin with destruction—is ritualized in the Jewish liturgy of Yom Kippur. It is this day, ritualized and thus repeated, that renders cyclical a process of generating novel recompositions. It expresses the discontinuity at the heart of the relationship between God and a people, such that destruction and creation never cease. According to Taubes, "it says—this Talmudically is the verse—on this day I will cover up all your sins: before God. Before the Lord you will be purified. So the day forgives."[29] The day, though in one sense like every other day, marks the otherness of days, much like the logic of the Sabbath day or year; there is an immanence of days, but also a discontinuity of days—a secularization of the apocalyptic. Whatever is accumulated over the course of days, whatever signification becomes regnant and appears to have the power to determine existence, is underdetermined by the signification of the Yom Kippur liturgy. On this day time itself emerges, a time that is innocent, for it does not mark the sovereignty or inner development of what is given. One could say that God excessively forgives, or alternatively that the namelessness of immanence frees time from the continuity of history by asserting itself against the fictions composed by signification—and it is not necessary

29. Ibid., 32.

to choose between these analyses, just as Spinoza did not need to choose between God or Nature.

Taubes enables us to see that it is precisely this dynamic that drives Pauline thought. When Paul makes Christ into a break with the law, when he conceives a radical transvaluation of the value set forth by the Powers, he is affirming the essential disequilibrium of relation to God, the discontinuity deeper than any established continuity of relation. This new people, which will come to bear the name of Christianity, is a people founded by discontinuity. The question, however, is whether it will remain a discontinuous people. There is, no doubt, a fundamental discontinuity involved in the Christian people insofar as it names the differential assemblage of Jew and Greek. But does not the name "Christian," this third term that mediates the discontinuity, end up producing its own insidious continuity?

Love

The establishment of a Christian people, and thus of Christianity, receives pressure not only from the apocalyptic disequilibrium that enables its invention, but also from the logic of love. It is well known that Paul, when surveying the virtues of faith, hope, and love, distinguishes the last from the former two insofar as it remains, eternally, even when the object of faith and hope is realized. Taubes, commenting on this presently hackneyed yet nonetheless central statement, pushes right to the heart of its logic. "Love means that I am not centered in myself . . . but rather: I have a need. The other person is needed. . . . The point in Paul is that even in perfection I am not an I, but we are a we."[30] In many ways, this Pauline injunction echoes Jesus's declaration of enemy-love. If the "I" perfects itself only in relation to a "we," then it is difficult to see how love can be anything other than limitless—unless, of course, the "we" is not universal but instead located within the bounds of the Christian community.

It is a question, then, of the level at which Paul's injunction is pitched. Is it an ethical maxim for those within the Christian community, or is it a practice that makes possible Christian existence? In other words, is love the way of being solely for those who are "inside" the Christian people, or is it something that, precisely insofar as it is directed "outside," irreducibly problematizes the very notion of an "inside"? It is certainly the

30. Ibid., 55–56.

case that Jesus's directive of enemy-love, which I have claimed belongs to the content of Christian declaration, would call for the latter interpretation—and there is no reason to presume that Paul saw himself as preaching something that would either add to or restrict the preaching of Jesus. If the "I" cannot be centered in itself, but must instead be composed through its affection by others, it seems that the "we," as well, should not be centered in itself, but must be constructed through its encounters with its exteriority. Love demands a differential form, it cannot be identitarian, for a we necessarily exceeds its own reflexive sedimentation, it is intrinsically excessive. In fact, is this not diasporic existence, to let one's own identifying signification be altered by the signification of the other, without a third term? Is it not to be deterritorialized without holding on to a pre-established invariance, and thus to compose something new? Only in this way would it be possible to say—to *become*—"we."

Yet the possibility of giving an identitarian form to "we" is not entirely foreclosed by Paul, and this is because the possibility of interpreting Christian peoplehood (whether in terms of communal or political existence) in terms of identity is not entirely foreclosed. To make one's identity contingent upon diasporic composition with the other is to put identity at risk; to foreground identity is to make diasporic composition impossible. Paul seems to wager on the side of the former, for in the same letter that he speaks of love he also asserts that "power is made perfect in weakness" (2 Cor 12:9)—and there is a real weakness in diaspora. The pragmatic difficulty occasioned by this weak power—or, really, the need to avoid such difficulty—seems, however, to have outweighed diasporic commitment. Thus, according to Daniel Bell's interpretation, the Augustinian theory of just war involves affirming that the violence one commits *is* an expression of love. Just wars are "born of the hope that evil persons might learn from the example of Christians what is to be valued truly and that through the patient goodwill of Christians they might be prompted to repent, reform, and restore the peace."[31] Violence, in other words, is not, as a figure such as Reinhold Niebuhr would have it, a tragic compromise of Christian declaration; it is rather the proper way of performing this declaration. As counterintuitive as Bell's claim may seem, it must be admitted that it is a consistent application of love, once love ceases to be a movement of deterritorialization and instead revolves around an established territory

31. Bell, *Just War as Christian Discipleship*, 30. My use of Bell here has been shaped by Ry O. Siggelkow's review, "Just War Is *Not* Christian Discipleship."

of Christian identity. Bell claims that "God created humanity to live in a just and peaceable community, and just wars are sometimes appropriate means of restoring and maintaining the tranquility of that order."[32] In such a scenario, Christianity becomes the arbiter of value, the agent that loves by ensuring the continuous deployment of social order. Love is given meaning by Christian discourse, rather than the other way around. We are far from the radical transvaluation of Paul's political theology, but perhaps less far from Paul's establishment of a Christian people.

Chaos

Paul's political theology unleashes chaos—or, at the very least, it unleashes something that must appear, in its refusal of law, as chaos to the Powers that resist it. This is to say that whatever it is that Paul advances is something that resides in the indeterminate, refusing as it does the dominant modes of determination. What is up in the air, then, is the direction that this apparently chaotic political theology should, or can, pursue. Is Pauline political theology to ally itself with a chaos that would form one side of a binary with order? Is it chaotic only relatively, but in itself bound to a different order? If this last is the case, then in what sense is such an order different in character from the order that it resists? My interest, given my argument thus far, is in the possibility of political theology that would pose chaos against the order of the Powers, and that would proceed neither to resolve itself in an alternative order—here we would have an analogy between the "Caesarian superego" and the "Christian superego"—nor to simply advocate chaos—for this would be to remain relative to the Powers, to be determined, even if chaotically, in virtue of the Powers. What is interesting, more precisely, is the possibility of loving chaos, and of doing so through diasporic composition.

It is here that Taubes's appreciative opposition to Schmitt becomes relevant. What is valuable in Schmitt is that he recognizes the force of apocalyptic; he understands that something becomes explicit in Pauline political theology, and this is that law *can* be opposed. Yet this is not to say that law *should* be opposed, and it is here that Schmitt departs from Taubes's Paul. Nonetheless, even if one opposes Pauline apocalyptic, it becomes clear that the very fact of Paul's antagonism towards law renders erroneous the idea that law reflects a natural order. In order to preserve law, one needs a political artifice of the theological, for Paul has already

32. Ibid., 28.

used this political-theological artifice in order to depose law. It is in this respect that one cannot ground law in a natural order, one cannot just be a jurist; one must ground law in the groundless political-theological artifice of the decision. When this is not done, the chaos that is there is able to outstrip order. Taubes remarks that the key Schmittian concept here is "the *katechon*: The retainer [*der Aufhalter*] that holds down the chaos that pushes up from below. That isn't my worldview, that isn't my experience. I can imagine as an apocalyptic: let it go down."[33] Note that this is a disagreement within the realm of the political-theological. There is no attempt to imagine apocalyptic as illusory; on the contrary, the apocalyptic renders illusory the idea that one could ignore it. It is in this regard that we should understand Schmitt's well known hatred of liberalism, which—much like the sort of cosmopolitan law that Paul opposes—seeks to create a continuous space of conversation, of dialogical harmonization. Apocalyptic cannot be thought by such an anti-theological politics, and thus the sheer thinkability of apocalyptic nullifies liberalism. Prior to any continuity of conversation there is the discontinuity of decision—a decision on what to do with the excess that chaos presents to law. Should this excess be allowed to disintegrate the Powers? If Taubes is appreciative of Schmitt, it is because Schmitt does not evade this question. It is with Schmitt in mind that Taubes says he is able to "understand that someone else is invested in this world and sees in the apocalypse, whatever its form, the adversary and does everything to keep it subjugated and suppressed, because from there forces can be unleashed that we are in no position to control."[34] Nonetheless, faced with the same question, Taubes decides otherwise, for he has "no spiritual investment in the world as it is."[35] Apocalyptic is discontinuous with the given world, so it is a matter either of inoculating oneself against this discontinuity or of affirming it.

Additionally, however, it might be possible to affirm apocalyptic in such a mode that one is simultaneously able to inoculate oneself—this could be done by deferring the realization of the apocalyptic to a future time, or by interiorizing the apocalyptic. In such instances, apocalyptic is affirmed, but as something that transcends the present. Its discontinuity is mapped onto a separation between the already and the not-yet, the flesh and the spirit, the material and the spiritual. When this takes place,

33. Taubes, *Political Theology of Paul*, 103.
34. Ibid.
35. Ibid.

partial hegemony is granted to the Powers, one cuts a deal between order and apocalyptic. Even Yoder, who tends to avoid any mediations of or compromises between Christian declaration and its object of antagonism, moderates this antagonism in his account of Paul's theory of the Powers. "It is important," Yoder says, "to begin with the reminder that they were part of the good creation of God. Society and history, even nature, would be impossible without regularity, system, order—and God has provided for this need."[36] Of course, in continuing he notes that the Powers, as we now know them, are "fallen," which is to say that they do not form an object of imitation. Still, "despite their fallenness," they "continue to exercise an ordering function. Even tyranny . . . is still better than chaos and we should be subject to it. The law . . . is nevertheless righteous and good and we should obey it."[37] What is interesting here is that, even amidst a radical refusal of the determination of the Powers, the promotion of the Powers remains. Why? Because they belong, as Schmitt said, to the *katechon*. In other words, despite the new community that Paul sees developing in those who adhere to Christian declaration, and despite the fundamental transvaluation of values effected by Paul's theory of Christ's relation to the law, one must still obey the Powers.

According to Yoder, there is no doubt that the Powers are fallen, that they are tainted in such a way that they must not be imitated, and that they are the object of political-theological antagonism. Nevertheless, they were here first—that is, they were created good, and so they maintain, even in their fallenness, the divinely established order. It is "important" to heed this "reminder," lest one get the idea that Christian declaration involves a decision on behalf of chaos against order, that it has "no spiritual investment in the world as it is." Even if Pauline apocalyptic brings chaos, such discontinuity will be synthesized by a restoration of ordering functions, now properly Christian. Or, failing an immediate Christian victory, one will have to make do, in the meantime, with God's providential use of unredeemed Powers, since they at least provide order, and since the true fulfillment of apocalyptic discontinuity is deferred. In the beginning, then, was order, and every failure of order is seen in this light, as if the problem were with the execution of order, rather than the nature of order. But what if what is second becomes first? What if, in other words, the chaotic discontinuity of apocalyptic, which comes *after* the order of the Powers,

36. Yoder, *Politics of Jesus*, 141.
37. Ibid.

which breaks with the law, is in fact a revelation that what is *before*, i.e., the originary order, is misbegotten? This would be to shift the focus from restoring, or maintaining in compromised form, an originary order, to composing differentially a world that would need neither order nor the constant reminder that order—even when tyrannical—is necessary.

How does one adjudicate which reading of Paul is to be preferred, and which decision is to be made? One certainly cannot do so by discovering the "true" interpretation of Paul, for elements affirmative of both order and chaos are there. Taubes, Schmitt, and Yoder, throughout their various disagreements and peculiar overlappings, all remain, in some meaningful sense, theoretical descendants of Paul—who is at once the thinker of *katechon* and the anarchic theorist of revolution against Rome. Accordingly, a Christianity shaped by the dialectical tension of order and chaos in Paul's thought is able not only to produce figures such as Marguerite Porete[38] and Thomas Müntzer, but also to call for their demise. Therefore, once again, it is not a question of reclaiming a purified Paul, but rather of understanding the tensions intrinsic to his thought and constructing new decisions on them.

World

What becomes of the world in Pauline thought? As Taubes notes, in an attempt to contextualize Hegel's *Weltgeist*, "there is such a thing as world-spirit; it exists as a polemical concept against Paul. Because Paul differentiates . . . between the *pneuma tou kosmou*, the *pneuma* of this world or of this eon as a negative concept, and *pneuma tou theou*, the spirit of God."[39] Yet even if the world is negative, it is also the materiality that is to be adjoined to the spirit of God. How is this possible—or, more to the point, can such a concept of the world sustain this bifurcating tension? Must there not be some kind of mediation? Indeed, it is precisely such mediation that Hegel provides by conceiving, as inherent in the world, both a destructive and an affirmative modality. While it is hard to imagine that Paul would agree with Hegel's account, it is equally hard to imagine this account apart from the pressure created by Paul's paradoxical account of the world. After all, when Hegel speaks of the world-spirit he is not

38. For a fascinating discussion of the anarchist potentialities of Porete's thought, and of how these stand outside the account of the political theology of Schmitt, see Critchley, "Mystical Anarchism," 272–306.

39. Taubes, *Political Theology of Paul*, 43.

simply affirming that which Paul opposes, he is rather seeking an implicit middle term between the anti-worldly spirit of God and the world that is to be redeemed. It is in this sense that Hegel remains within the ambit of Christianity. Yet I mention Hegel here not to advocate for his specific manner of mediation but instead to highlight the intrinsically problematic character of the concept of the world. This is to say that I see Hegelian logic less as a break with the tensions of Pauline thought (as Taubes may be understood to suggest), and more as a symptom of them. For me, what is more compelling than a Hegelian reconciliation of Paul's tensions is the possibility of making these tensions into something that would problematize Paul's thought itself. The central difficulty that Paul creates for himself can, I believe, be traced to the radically political character of his theology, which, due to the absoluteness of its stand against Rome, calls for an affirmation of apocalyptic discontinuity so profound that only a concept such as the world can do justice to the totality of its enemy. Once this move has been made, however, the centrality of the world—as constitutive material—to liberation is disregarded. Douglas Harink indicates this loss of the world when he contends that "in Paul the apocalypse of Jesus Christ is indeed a world-dissolving and world-constituting event."[40] What is left out of such a formulation is the *matter* of the world: it is the middle term of the opposition between dissolution and constitution, it is that without which both would be unthinkable, yet it remains unthought in itself.

In order to make sense of this paradox whereby the world functions, from a transcendent vantage, as the object of antagonism (or something to be dissolved), but also, still, as something to be redeemed (or at least newly constituted), we should make reference to the reading of Paul advanced by Daniel Boyarin's *A Radical Jew*.[41] According to Boyarin, Paul's thought is motivated by the desire for universalization, and this motivation is so fundamental that the entirety of his thought should be interpreted according to this cipher. Such an impetus towards the universal does not, of course, happen in a vacuum; it emerges out of a Jewish context in which it is asked whether the God of all creation should be concerned solely with a particular people. What Paul saw in Christ, then, was a way of satisfactorily addressing the tension between particularity

40. Harink, *Paul Among the Postliberals*, 50. It may very well be the case that this lacuna in Pauline thought sets the stage for the later emergence of a self-consciously secular manner of thinking.

41. Boyarin, *Radical Jew*, 13–15.

and universality, a way of articulating, at one and the same time, the truth of God's election of the Jewish people and the necessity of this election becoming universalized.

The manner in which Paul holds together the two poles of this tension is allegory. It should be noted, first of all, that this is not the sort of allegory that will later be found in a figure such as Origen. Pauline allegory is concerned not with deciphering detailed signifying relations between the literal and spiritual meanings, but rather with establishing the two-tiered structure of allegory as such—thus, while there is no Origen without Paul, Paul's interests do not coincide with Origen's. Paul's aim, more broadly, is to move from the particular to the universal, and he does so by moving from the literal to the spiritual, which is also to move from the material to the spiritual.[42] "Allegory" therefore does not refer only to a specified mode of reading texts, but more expansively to a way of understanding the world (or the relation between God and the world). The "universal humanity" sought by Paul "was predicated (and still is) on the dualism of the flesh and the spirit, such that while the body is particular, marked through practice as Jew or Greek, and through anatomy as male or female, the spirit is universal."[43] If one wants to bring about a process of unification, it will be difficult to do so insofar as there are irreducible material differences. Accordingly, in order to evade the obstacle of irreducibility, it will be necessary to cast universality at a level beyond the one inhabited by difference. This is the need to which Paul's dualism answers.

Nonetheless, even as there is a hierarchy within this dualism—one in which spirit transcends flesh—this does not mean flesh is destroyed. As Boyarin continues, "Paul did not, however, reject the body—as did, for instance, the Gnostics—but rather promoted a system whereby the body had its place, albeit subordinated to the spirit."[44] The body, or the material, is not denied so much as preserved and subordinated—and there are resonances here with Hegel's sublation—to the spirit. What we have, then, is a dualism that is not only ontological but also anthropological. Boyarin adds to these two a "hermeneutical dualism" (he sometimes calls this an "epistemological dualism"): "Just as the human being is divided into a fleshy and a spiritual component, so also is language itself. It is composed

42. For a discussion by Boyarin of Pauline allegory's relationship to Patristic allegory, as well as to the thought of Philo, see ibid., 13–15.

43. Ibid., 7.

44. Ibid.

of outer, material signs and inner, spiritual significations."[45] This way of understanding Scripture and the world is equally a way of understanding the relationship between particular Jewish existence and the universal Christian existence that he is constructing. As Boyarin says, "the physical, fleshy signs of the Torah, of historical Judaism, are re-interpreted as symbols of that which Paul takes to be universal requirements and possibilities for humanity."[46] Israel according to the flesh gives way to—is preserved by being subordinated to—Israel according to the spirit, in other words the new Christian people. This progression is exemplified most directly by the claim that circumcision is no longer necessary to become part of the universal people, the people that includes both Jews and Greeks, for this people exists at the level of the spirit, where there is *neither* Jew *nor* Greek. Circumcision of the flesh gives way to circumcision of the heart. Of course, it should be said—though it may be obvious—that the ontological, anthropological, and hermeneutical dualisms are made possible through the Christological dualism: "just as Christ had a physical nature and a spiritual nature (Romans 9:5), and both are valuable, though the former is subordinate to the latter, so also the physical observances of the Torah and the people of Israel."[47] In other words, there is not so much an eclipse of the Torah and of particular, material Jewish existence as a fulfillment, in the person of Christ, of their spiritual—that is, allegorical—meaning, which was there all along, though only revealed in the coming of Christ. Indeed, it is precisely this revelation that makes up the event of apocalypse for Boyarin's Paul. The apocalyptic revelation of Christ is given sense by an allegorical structure; this structure allows Christ to reveal something that is discontinuous with what came before, but that is also the fulfillment—allegorically speaking—of what came before.

The brevity of my summation does not do justice to the richness of Boyarin's argument, but it does advance the purpose of this section, which is to examine the juxtaposition, in Pauline thought, of a world both judged and redeemed. When Paul names the spirit of the world as his enemy, he is speaking at the level of transcendence. The Powers, which give determinacy to the spirit of the world, are an obstacle to the unification of humanity that is revealed in Christ; they are in absolute discontinuity with what is apocalyptically revealed. This antagonism with the Powers is irre-

45. Ibid.
46. Ibid.
47. Ibid., 29.

ducible, then, because the Powers determine a world in which difference is irreducible. If there is to be unity or universality then it must, by definition, be One, and Christ is the One that admits no difference.[48] But what then happens to the world? How can Paul's antagonism towards the world also enable the redemption of the world? It can do so allegorically, which is to say that it can do so by subordinating the world to the apocalyptic revelation of Christ. The world is not redeemed in its worldliness, but it is redeemed insofar as it is subordinated to the spirit of Christ. It is hard not to discern in this the previously mentioned battle of the superegos— that is, the replacement of the Powers' transcendent determination of the world with Christ's transcendent determination of the world. Of course, Paul, according to Boyarin's reading, would respond that the world, in order to be what it always was, or always was meant to be, must participate allegorically in Christ. But this begs the question of materiality that does not participate—and even more to the point, of materiality that seeks to remain material, that does not wish to give up its particularity in order to realize itself in Christian universality. Boyarin has specifically in mind Jewish existence, which would need to cease being Jewish, or to cease defining itself by its particular, material way of being Jewish, in order to become universal. What also come to mind, though, are the countless peoples that, in the historical course of Christian mission, or conquest, have been "called" to subordinate their particular, material ways of being in order to enter into the universal people.

It is here, then, that the question of the world emerges problematically. What happens to the world, understood materially, and thus particularly—differentially—when it passes through Pauline thought? On one hand, there is no need to dismiss a priori the desire for commonality, for a solidarity that would not be delimited by oppositions, but, on the other, it remains difficult to see value in a transcendent universality that would value a differential world only insofar as it is allegorically subordinated

48. Boyarin's account of the interconnection between the desire for a universality of the One and the refusal of the materiality of Jewish existence is exemplified in the modern period by the link Kant makes between the "euthanasia of Judaism" and the hope for "one shepherd and one flock." Kant says: "The euthanasia of Judaism is pure moral religion, freed from all the ancient statutory teachings, some of which were bound to be retained in Christianity (as a messianic faith). But this division of sects, too, must disappear in time, leading, at least in spirit, to what we call the conclusion of the great drama of religious change on earth (the restoration of all things), when there will be only one shepherd and one flock." See Kant, *Conflict of the Faculties*, 95.

to the universal of Christ. Once again, the possibility of understanding apocalyptic through the lens of diaspora becomes helpful, for when this is done worldly difference is not something to be allegorically overcome, but something that composes, precisely *as* difference, a redeemed world. For diaspora, the particularizing character of signification is not an obstacle to allegorical universalization, it is rather the material potentiality of interparticularity, of differential composition. We are able to say, having looked at Paul's account of law, people, chaos, and world, that Pauline thought, in the end, does not advocate diaspora. This does not mean Pauline thought must be avoided—indeed, we have done something different, which is to track the way that diaspora is foreclosed in Paul, as well as the way that diaspora remains hidden, at least as a potentiality, within his thought.

Immanence is productive, which is to say that it is necessarily generative, even as what it happens to generate is not necessary—what is necessary is only that immanence happens. At the same time, there is no doubt that one of the most "significant" happenings of immanence is adumbrated under Pauline thought. Let us recall that immanence is properly nameless, but it always doubles itself, such that every attempt to properly name immanence will be immanently exceeded. Signification is necessary because of this excessive production of immanence, but signification will always be fictive or improper. This means that signification, though contingent, is central to the production of immanence. We are never bound by the limits of signification, for immanence is properly nameless, but we can undo these limits only by understanding and undoing accumulated signification. This is an act of resistance, but a resistance that, in its decompositional and recompositional modalities, is able to create from an immanence that was never mastered by previously existing signification. It is this logic that must be kept in mind as we move beyond this chapter on Pauline thought, and as we observe the significance of Paul for the present. Just as psychoanalysis teaches us that when we speak, it may very well be not our voice at work but one (or more) of the many voices we have heard, so when we think today it may be the thought of Paul that courses through our brain. It is good to consider this possibility—not in order to return to our Pauline origins, nor to wipe clean Paul's echo, but merely to navigate with more sophistication the way in which we construct the future.

Of course, even if we accept that Pauline thought has been quite significant for the historical processes that have accumulated previous to the present, it must equally be admitted that other significations have happened, also in the wake of Paul yet just as determinative of the present. We must track the signification of Pauline thought, but we also must track other innovative significations of immanent surplus; we no longer live in a hegemonically Christian epoch, but we do live in what Charles Taylor has notably called "a secular age."[49] In fact, as much as I have sought to limn the import of Pauline thought, it might also be possible to see such thought merely as the pre-history of the secular. Accordingly, the aims of this chapter will be continued into the next, but the theme will shift from one dominant mode of signification to another: from the concepts of Paul to the concept of the secular and of its adjunct, the concept of religion.

49. Taylor, *A Secular Age.*

4

Christianity, Religion, and the Secular

There is no longer Jew or Greek, there is no longer slave or free, there is no longer male and female; for all of you are one in Christ Jesus.

—Paul[1]

This notion that identity is achieved and not given by birth, history, language, and geographical location was the novum that produced religion.

—Daniel Boyarin[2]

Most important, then, secularism is a name Christianity gave itself when it invented "religion," named its other or others as "religions."

—Gil Anidjar[3]

O NE OF THE PROMINENT features of Pauline thought, as analyzed in the previous chapter, was its attempt to conceive a new people. It is this "project" that provides a link between Paul and the contemporary discursive regime—even though the latter is primarily shaped by the

1. Gal 3:28.
2. Boyarin, *Border Lines*, 17.
3. Anidjar, *Semites*, 48.

concepts of "religion" and "the secular," the relation of which remains out-side the ambit of Pauline thought as such, the invention of these concepts occurs in a milieu generated by Paul. Putting this more directly, we can say that Paul's conception of a new people—that is, of Christianity (even though this name is not yet explicit in Paul)—is coeval with the concep-tion of something called "religion," and that the shift that leads to our contemporary discourse on religion and the secular occurs against this background. Our present milieu, then, is not properly Pauline, but it is unthinkable apart from Pauline thought; it is a selection of one possible path among many made available by Paul. The aim of the present chapter is to track this development, from the Christian invention of religion to the modern opposition between religion and the secular, and to argue that what is consistently precluded is the sort of movement that I have called diaspora. I will argue, concomitantly, that resistance to this development requires not the foregrounding of one of these three terms (Christianity, religion, or the secular) against the others, but rather the refraction of all of them—that is, a decomposition and recomposition of them—in virtue of a constructive concept of diaspora.

The Christian Invention of Religion

Paul's challenge, I have argued, was to find a way to understand the nature of the people that was becoming constituted in the wake of the gospel of Christ. His existential involvement in the mission to the Gentiles made this task exert a special pressure on his thought: What was to be made of this community that, while born out of Jewish existence, was becom-ing increasingly Gentile, or "Greek"? That this was a complex, wrenching question for Paul is evident from the dialectically taut ruminations of Romans 9–11. Taubes, we have seen, discerns in Paul's thought a repeti-tion of Moses's wrestling over the potentiality for God to destroy and to create a people. Even granting this principle, however, we must address the specific nature of the Christian community—yes, it emerges out of the discontinuous, out of an apocalyptic relation to a God that is other to ev-ery given reality, but the question still remains of how this new, apocalyp-tic people holds together. Paul's very direct answer, we have seen, is that this people is neither Jew nor Greek, and that this is precisely because this people is "in Christ." It is here, then, that we find not the explicit name, but certainly the conceptual lineaments, of religion. What, one must ask, is this community that is in Christ? Is it something analogous to Jewish existence and Greek existence, such that existence in Christ provides a third species for a common genus? This is a difficult interpretation to accept, for it does not seem to account for Paul's sense of the novelty of being in Christ, the sense in which existence in Christ belongs to a different order than the existence one has by belonging to a people by birth. Accordingly, it is more compelling to turn to the allegorical structure of Paul's thought: when we speak of Jewish or Greek existence, we are speaking of the flesh; when we speak of existence in Christ, we are speaking of the spirit. It is here, then, in Pauline thought's allegorical structure, with its separation of existence according to flesh from existence according to the spirit, that we find the conceptual outline of what will be called religion.

This new people that is in Christ, that is essentially identified by belonging to Christ—that will eventually come to be called the Christian people, and that will become part of that religion of Christianity—is a people of the spirit. There will still be "cultic" practices, of course, for to belong to the spirit is not simply to negate the material. Nonetheless, material practices and identifications of the flesh will cease to be determinative. The material plane will be superseded by its allegorical participation in the spiritual plane. It is this innovation—in other words, the construction of an additional plane, beyond that of the material—that makes necessary a novel concept, the concept of religion. Of course, this is not to say that there was no word, or even concept, of religion already in existence. It is to say, however, that this word is given a new meaning, that religion undergoes a fundamental shift, and that what emerges from this shift is significantly different from what was already in place. Religion no longer names the practices that mediate a certain ethno-cultural existence; it begins instead to name one's relation to a newly born spiritual plane.

This shift is nicely demonstrated by Richard King, who notes that prior to Christianity *religio* was "virtually synonymous with *traditio*," and that "it represented the teachings of one's ancestors and was essentially not open to question."[4] This means, he continues, that one could not be right or wrong about religion, for religion was not a matter of truth or falsity. Religion, in short, was a matter of belonging to a tradition, of being habituated to and within a given cultural existence. It should be clear why this definition of religion would pose an obstacle to Christian existence, which was predicated on the idea that one's identity was derived

4. King, *Orientalism and Religion*, 35.

not from one's cultural tradition—Jewish or Greek existence—but from one's willed adherence to Christ. The shift in the meaning of religion is thus produced by the emergence of Christianity. According to King, "It became increasingly important within early Christian discourses to drive a wedge between the traditional association of *religio* with *traditio*."[5] As an example of this intervention, King cites Lactantius, a third-century CE Christian, who asserts that religion "is a worship of the true; superstition of the false. . . . They are superstitious who worship many and false gods; but we, who supplicate the one true God, are religious."[6] Religion is thus delinked from cultural givenness, from the material singularities of tradition, and relocated on a spiritual plane, such that it concerns the relation to the true God as revealed in Christ.

Pauline universalism cannot accommodate a plurality of religious traditions, at least not insofar as these are ultimately determinative of identity. Similarly, the new people of Christ cannot be yet another religion, insofar as religion refers to particular cultural practices. The only way forward is to remake religion in the image of Christianity. This, according to Boyarin, is what happened amongst Gentile Christians "who were not prepared (for whatever reason) to think of themselves as Jews," and it began to happen "as early as the second century, if not at the end of the first."[7] What happened, specifically, was the decision to pursue "the option of seeing *Christianismos* as an entirely novel form of identity."[8] What was decided, in other words, was to make Christianity belong to an entirely new category, religion, such that the invention of Christianity amounts to the invention of religion, and vice versa. In order to render this category novel, however, some distinctive characteristic must be provided, a characteristic that makes something count as religion, rather than as something else. This distinctive characteristic, Boyarin observes, is belief, and so the distinctive characteristic of *true* religion is *right* belief—in other words, orthodoxy. Christianity, as it becomes a new kind of identity, carries with it a new way of defining identity.[9] For the inventors of

5. Ibid., 36.

6. Ibid.

7. Boyarin, *Border Lines*, 16–17.

8. Ibid., 17.

9. Denise Kimber Buell, in *Why This New Race*, makes an argument that somewhat complicates this statement, but that does not ultimately contradict it. Specifically, Buell wants to challenge the presupposition that the Christian/Jewish difference can be mapped onto the opposition between non-ethnic and ethnic, or between religion and race. She

Christianity, "the question of who's in and who's out became the primary

aims to "challenge the view that ethnicity and race were irrelevant to early Christians" (x), and claims, for instance, that "Even if one wants to insist that being a member of some 'Christian people' is qualitatively different than being Jewish, Greek, Roman, Egyptian, and so on, it is not sufficient to state that Christians formed a 'religion' in contrast to a 'race' or 'ethnicity.' Many early Christians described the consequences of belief in Christ (even though the kinds of belief varied widely) as acquiring membership in a people. When various believers in and followers of Christ (however understood) used ethnic reasoning, they were continuing a longstanding practice of viewing religious practices and beliefs as intertwined with collective identifications that overlap with our modern concepts of race and ethnicity, as well as nationality and civic identity" (166). I am in agreement with this line of argumentation. Indeed, one of the main points I take from her groundbreaking book is the real difference between early Christian notions of identity and modern Christian (or post-Christian secular) notions of identity. Though in each case the claim to superiority is articulated in virtue of a connection to an anti-Jewish universality that is elsewhere lacking, the nature of this connection is not homologous. The modern Christian (or post-Christian secular) universality claims to have delinked itself from all ethnoracial characteristics, but the early Christian universality is inseparable from a peculiar affirmation of ethnoracial characteristics.

Yet this raises a fundamental question: if early Christian identity is articulated in relation to ethnoracial reasoning, then is not Christianity yet another particularity? If Christianity interweaves religious discourse with ethnoracial discourse, then in what sense can it be said that Christianity engenders a distinctive concept of religion? It is under the pressure of such questions that I must emphasize what I have just referred to as Christianity's "peculiar" affirmation of ethnoracial discourse. Buell adverts to this peculiar appropriation by observing, in her reading of Justin Martyr, that he "does not reject but rather redefines the concept of ethnoracial membership for Christians" (98). It is the *redefinition* of ethnoracial discourse that points to the novelty of the Christian concept of religion. In other words, if the argument for the Christian invention of religion depended on the mutual exclusivity of religion and ethnoracial discourse, then Buell's successful demonstration of the ethnoracial dimension in Christian religion's self-articulation would refute the argument. What I want to clarify, however, is that the argument has no such dependence on a mutually exclusive binary between religious and ethnoracial discourse. The novelty of Christian religion resides, quite precisely, in the refiguration of the relation between religion and ethnoraciality: Christian identity most certainly has to do with peoplehood, but, more to the point, it has to do with the imagination of a people (or an ethnoracial community) whose *religion* enables it to go beyond the limits of other peoples. It is not that Christians are not a people; it is rather that they are a people that is not like the other peoples. Buell is in accord with these distinctions, I believe, when she remarks: "Justin resituates the notion of an ethnoracial essence (something 'fixed') by defining faith, not blood, as the essence of Christianness. It is the conceptualization of peoplehood that undergoes transformation, not the notion of membership in a people" (98). And further on, when explaining—in Justin's thought—how the Christian people distinguishes itself from the Jewish people as the universal from the particular, she observes that "the particular is construed as limited and temporally bound ('fixed'), whereas the universal is construed as eternal and more fluid, because anyone can adopt the universal law and join the universal people" (110). In this latter citation, then, Christianity appears as fluid, whereas in the former citation it appears as fixed. Buell rightly points to the interplay of fluidity and fixity in way of thinking about Christianicity. The vehicle to answer that question was, again for these Christians, orthodoxy and heresy. 'In' was to be defined by correct belief; 'out' by adherence via an alleged choice to false belief."[10] Furthermore, the definition of religion in terms of belief (rather than in terms, say, of ethnocultural practice) means that religious identity becomes something to be achieved, rather than something that is given. One's identity comes not from material determinants but from what one chooses to believe. Boyarin thus remarks that the "notion that identity is achieved and not given by birth, history, language, and geographical location was the novum that produced religion."[11]

What I would like to foreground about Boyarin's account is the fundamentally dialectical character of the constitution of Christianity. That is, in order for a thing called Christianity to emerge, there must likewise emerge things that are not Christianity. What becomes inescapable is a binary opposition between Christianity and its outside, and this binary is dialectical insofar as Christianity, in order to name its identity, must also name what falls short of this identity. Christianity constitutes itself by constituting its others—its enemies, in fact. This happens, first, through what Boyarin calls "heresiology," understood as the simultaneous determination and devalorization of beliefs that depart from, or inadequately

---

Christian religion's ethnoracial reasoning. What I would add is that it is the way in which these function together—fixity granting ethnocultural identity, fluidity granting to such an identified people a universality lacking from other peoples—that marks the novelty of Christianity's self-understanding, and thus of its concept of religion. Indeed, Buell says that "Early Christian texts could foreground fixity to negotiate change, either by appealing to restoration of ancient practices or continuity of descent, but they could also highlight ethnic fluidity while nonetheless presupposing a kind of common essence to humanity," such that Christians could imagine themselves "as belonging to a people who had realized humanity's 'true' potential" (78). Even as the Christian people emerges, in one instance, on the same plane as other peoples, it does so only as it converges—in a way that other peoples do not—with a separate, overarching plane of universality. Thus Buell describes one of Clement's theses as follows: "The universalizing potential of the category 'Christian' . . . implicitly positions 'Hellene' and 'Jew' as finite and inferior" (140). Therefore, while the invention of Christianity and of religion is linked to the invention of a people, and in this sense to a "pre-Christian" account of religion, it nonetheless occasions a fundamental break by injecting religion with a non-preexisting valence, and this is precisely because of the way it submits the concept of peoplehood to a "transformation" whereby a (Christian) people's religion makes it not just another people, but on the contrary "the universal people," or the people who have "realized humanity's 'true' potential."

10. Boyarin, *Border Lines*, 17.

11. Ibid.

remain faithful to, the proper belief.[12] In order for orthodoxy to exist, heterodoxy must also exist. Right belief has no meaning unless it is opposed to wrong belief, such that these come into existence coevally; orthodoxy posits itself by negating heterodoxy. This is how identity is given to *Christianity*. But how is identity given to Christianity *as religion*? If the invention of Christianity is also the invention of religion, then there is a co-implication between the identification of Christianity and the identification of religious truth. Christianity is, of course, marked as the truth of religion, but Christianity can identify itself in terms of true belief only if there is at the same time a category of religion whose goal is true belief. This is to say, then, that Christianity needs not only heresies, but also other religions. After all, if the Christian religion is true, there must be other religions that are false—otherwise Christian truth has no meaning except as a singularity among singularities. If there are no non-Christian religions, then Christianity's religious claim to truth has no validity for those outside Christianity. Consequently, the identification of Christian religious truth is in dialectical need not only of Christian heresy, but also of religious error.

It is in virtue of this need, Boyarin argues, that the invention of Christianity and of religion calls for the invention of Judaism *as a determinate religion*. My interest here is to highlight Christian religion's need for other religions as such, rather than the specific construction of something called Judaism. In fact, early Christianity will construct not just the religion of Judaism, but also of Hellenism. Nonetheless, given Christianity's origins, it cannot be doubted that it finds the constitution of Judaism as a rival religion to be a particularly pressing task. At the level of historical genesis, Christianity would seem to be derivative, and so the invocation of a plane of religious truth allows Christianity to present itself as, on the contrary, originary. It is subsequent at the level of history, but antecedent at the level of religion. Yet for this to work, Judaism must also be understood at the level of religion—if it is not a religion, then it cannot enter into comparison, and if it cannot enter into comparison, then it

12. As Boyarin puts it (*Border Lines*, xi–xiii): "I am arguing . . . that 'heresiology,' the extraordinary practice of anatomizing, pinning down, making taxonomies of Christians who are not somehow 'in,' was an integral part of the answer to the question, What kind of a thing will Christianity be? Integral to that heresiological answer as well was a response to Jews who would not be Christians, or, better put . . . a response to the question of how the mapping of a border with something that Christianity will call Judaism will make the new Christian self-definition as a 'religion' work."

cannot be identified as lacking. What is therefore at stake in the Christian invention of religion is a massive act of interpellation. Christianity calls itself into being, but in order to do so it must be positioned (eminently) within a larger field of heresies and other religions. That which is outside Christianity—whether as heresy or as other religion—must be positioned by, or in relation to, Christianity. Christianity's others cannot be allowed to position themselves autonomously, they must be positioned by Christianity even as they refuse Christianity, for only in this way can a field be constituted in which Christianity is hegemonic. This is what is meant by saying that interpellation is at work: even as something departs from Christianity, it must be called, or named, as that which falls short of Christianity. Everything does not need to become Christian, but everything does need to *aspire* to Christianity (or to what Christianity fully exemplifies)—and it is not just a matter of aspiring to Christian orthodoxy, it is also a matter of aspiring, temporally, to move beyond one's given identity (Jew or Greek) and to achieve Christian identity.

This installation of aspiration is precisely what is at work in the interpellation of Judaism—that is, the name-calling of Jewish existence as religion. It may be countered that Christianity cannot be the catalyst for the invention of Judaism, given that Jewish existence far preceded the emergence of Christianity. The point, however, is not that Jewish existence begins with the invention of Christianity, but rather that the interpellation of Jewish existence as a *religion* called Judaism commences with the Christian invention of religion. Such a point is made by Schwartz, who, on the basis of his historical investigations, contends that "one of the main causes of the rejudaization of the Jews was the christianizaton of the Roman Empire."[13] Furthermore, Boyarin, from whom I take the inspiration to see the constitution of Judaism (and other non-Christian religions) in terms of interpellation, observes that "it seems highly significant that there is no word in pre-modern Jewish parlance that means 'Judaism.' When the term *Ioudaismos* appears in non-Christian Jewish writing—to my knowledge only in 2 Maccabees—it doesn't mean Judaism the religion but the entire complex of loyalties and practices that mark off the people of Israel."[14] It is thus the work of Christianity to name Judaism as a religion, and, insofar as Christian religion became historically hegemonic, this appellation became inescapable. Yet even as the naming

13. Schwartz, *Imperialism and Jewish Society*, 179.
14. Boyarin, *Border Lines*, 8.

enacted by interpellation becomes inevitable, it is still possible to resist this name, or to make the name function otherwise. This, in fact, is precisely what Boyarin claims took place with Judaism. To belong to Judaism is to belong to a religion, but what kind of a religion is Judaism? It is, in short, a religion that seeks not to be one, and this is because it refuses the distinctive marks of religion as defined by Christianity: heresiology, along with the idea that identity is achieved rather than given.[15] One cannot become a Jewish heretic, nor can one lose one's Jewish identity by believing the wrong thing—and this is because Jewish identity, even when it is cast in the image of Christianity, is a given rather than an achieved identity. Judaism, on Boyarin's account, resists its interpellation, it makes its determination as religion into a condition of possibility for finding novel paths of its own desire.

Disembedding Religion

How, it may be asked, does a diasporic approach address this Christian invention of religion? It should be remarked, right away, that it does not recognize in this process of invention a diasporic version of Christianity. What is chosen here is not a path whereby enactment of Christian declaration calls for the composition of differential forms. On the contrary, Christianity here amounts to an identitarian form, one that defines itself through dialectical opposition to other identitarian forms—even to the point of encouraging such other forms to come into existence. Furthermore, this refusal of differential composition is imbricated in the refusal of immanence. The invention of religion amounts to the installation of transcendence—the transcendence of belief to material particularity, or of achieved spiritual identity to given material identity. A diasporic approach emphasizes that what is left out of such religion is material singularity, the difference of particularity. Boyarin has shown that it is precisely this material singularity, or particular difference, that Judaism emphasizes in order to resist the interpellation by Christian religion. Diaspora would

15. Boyarin claims that even as Judaism "appropriated" much from an emergent Christianity—and here he is following Schwartz—this appropriation must be understood "as a kind of mimicry in the technical postcolonial sense and thus as an act of resistance." This is to say that ultimately "rabbinic Judaism refused the option of becoming a religion, another species of the kind that Christianity offered. At the final stage of the development of classical rabbinism, a reassertion of the 'locative' of identity as given and not as achieved—or lost—came to be emblematic of Judaism." See *Border Lines*, 12.

involve, in addition to this emphasis on material singularity, the affirmation of interparticularity. This is to say that the initial resistance of material singularity to the transcendent identity of religion may be extended through interparticular composition.

The importance of diasporic interparticularity becomes prominent when we note Schwartz's claim that the Christian invention of religion involves a process of "disembedding." He remarks that Christianization's "sibling," in "social-historical terms," was "the emergence of religion as a discrete category of human experience," such that we may speak of "religion's *disembedding*."[16] Religion, in other words, functions as a deterritorializing agent, for it allows one to conceive oneself in a way that departs from one's immediate, or given, context—in this sense, religion provides a means of becoming-other. This deterritorializating movement of religion's disembedding therefore involves a real potentiality; it can be seen as the decompositional agent that enables the diasporic composition of novel, differential forms. Note, however, that the novelty of such forms would arise precisely from their differential character. They would be novel not because they adhere to the true, transcendent religion, but because they use religion as a mode of decomposing given identities and thus making possible differential relations. Religion would figure here not as something that stands above and beyond material particularity, but rather as something that traverses material particularities, desedimenting them and opening up compositional spaces in the cracks of identity. All of this is to highlight the diasporic potentiality of religion's disembedding. In fact, the radicality of Paul's political theology belongs to this potentiality, for it was precisely his "religious" account of Christ that enabled him to break with—to deterritorialize—the totality of Roman dominance. The summation of all things in the onto-juridical determination of Roman power was undone by the disembedding of "religious" value from its imperial context. This, in itself, is a positive indication of a profound capacity. It errs not in the discontinuity it introduces, but more precisely in its resolution of this discontinuity in a new version of transcendent dominology. We might say that Pauline thought deterritorializes potentiality from Roman imperial territory, but that it then gives rise to Christian religion, which by means of reterritorialization captures and forecloses this potentiality. Christian religion, though it is the heir of discontinuity,

16. Schwartz, *Imperialism and Jewish Society*, 179.

refuses to affirm this discontinuity when it conceives its relation to the differences of material particularity.

Diaspora stands against this tendency by refusing the refusal of material particularity, by seeing discontinuity as a constructive principle, rather than as the dialectical binary between Christian identity, on one hand, and heresy and rival religions, on the other. Instead of the transcendence of Christian religion, there must be an immanence of apocalyptic, decompositional discontinuity, and diasporic, creative recomposition of material particularities. When this sort of immanence is pursued, it becomes possible for religion to operate *problematically*, such that religion would function as something like a nomadic agent of otherness. Religion becomes that which disembeds, not in order to simply negate all formations but in order to compose differential forms. Disembedding is thus delinked from transcendent embedding, and freed for interparticular composition. Religion's disembedding would enable heteroglossia, or the ability to let the signification of others condition my own signification in a diasporic mimesis. In short, religion would name not Christian identity and its placement of its determinate others, but rather the nonidentity of material particularity and its displacing relations to other material particularities—the between of immanent becoming, rather than the achievement of transcendent identity. This is to affirm that religion's disembedding stems from the namelessness of immanence, and that it makes possible the novel production of mutually mimetic—or interparticular—significations. Signals get crossed in a kind of Babel, the value of which emerges in relation not to a lost measure of unity but rather to the immeasurability of immanent surplus.

Of course, the potentiality of religion that I am essaying is just that—a potentiality that remains as an alternative historical possibility, but certainly not as the hegemonic path of historical actualization. The concept of religion that became prominent was the concept with which I began the chapter—Christian religion. What religion came to mean, in other words, was not the immeasurable but rather the measure of Christianity. In fact, what is striking is that even amidst disembedding it seems to have become exigent, at least for certain Christians whose thought would gain dominance, that religion function to generate fixed boundaries. Measurability must be maintained—there must be an identifiable thing called Christianity, along with identifiable others such as Judaism and Hellenism, and these all must be identifiable as something called religion.

Anything that exceeds these bounded identities, anything that diasporically mixes with and mimes its other too much, cannot count as religion.
Indeed, Boyarin's own scholarly effort can be understood as being exerted
in the name of those who did not, or who refused to, adhere to identities
in accord with the "border lines."[17] What, then, is the promise of religion,
if religion has been formed according to the measure, or the border lines,
engendered by the invention of an identitarian Christianity? Boyarin
would emphasize the creative capacity that emerges in interpellation, and
it is in this vein that he cites Judith Butler's contention that, "In being
called an injurious name, one is derogated and demeaned. But the name
holds out another possibility as well: by being called a name, one is also,
paradoxically, given a certain possibility for social existence, initiated into
a temporal life of language that exceeds the prior purposes that animate
that call."[18] The theory of immanence that I am advancing would affirm
both the inevitability—or, more precisely, the irreversibility—of interpellation and the capacity to exercise creativity beneath and through such
name-calling. It would add, however, that what takes place in interpellation and its resistance should be understood in the context of immanence's proper namelessness and the necessity of fictive signification, the
co-implication of which articulates surplus. In other words, there will be
interpellation because there must be signification, and this interpellation
will always be ideological because signification is necessarily fictive. Fictive
signification, however, is the production of immanence, and so while it
can give rise to relations that are unhappy, it can also become the means
by which these unhappy relations are decomposed. There is, in short,
an ontological capacity—the surplus of the production of immanence,
which in its namelessness never signifies itself, but which for the very
same reason is irreducible to even the most dominant signification—that
allows us not just to subvert the names that are interpellatively imposed,
but also to excessively construct new names. Indeed, it may very well be

---

17. "Christian discourse from the second through the fifth centuries . . . kept producing a species of heretics called 'Jews' and 'Judaizers,' hybrids, 'monsters' to use the
terminology of one of the earliest of Christian writers, Ignatius of Antioch. . . . These
very monsters were to appear as a heresiological topos of the orthodox Christian writers
who almost constantly figured heresy as a hydra. The Rabbis, in those same centuries,
produced an analogous response, a discourse as well of the pure and the authentic opposed to the impure, the contaminated, the hybrid, the *min*. I speak here, then, for the
monsters" (Boyarin, *Border Lines*, xii).

18. Boyarin, *Border Lines*, 9.

said that religion, through its process of disembedding, exercised this constructive capacity. Accordingly, it is important for us to imagine, as I have just done above, this potentiality of religion to function diasporically and immanently.

Nonetheless, this opposition between religion as diasporic immanence and religion as Christian transcendence is only a beginning, for the history of the concept of religion extends well beyond its Christian invention—as I mentioned in commencing this chapter, the concept of diaspora requires a rethinking not merely of religion, but of the complex relation between religion, Christianity, and the secular. I have, in order to imagine what exceeds the Christian invention of religion, imagined an alternative account of religion; some, however, would claim that the means of liberating immanent surplus from religion's transcendence is found in the secular. This latter impulse has, in fact, been one pursued by a large segment of modern thought. A diasporic approach allows us to see genuine promise in this strategy, but it likewise allows us to discern a certain repetition of the Christian invention of religion in the modern invention of the secular.

The Invention of the Secular

Just as we can speak of a Christian invention of religion, so we can speak of an invention of the secular.[19] In each case, what is at stake is the construction not only of a position of judgment, but also of a plane of reality

---

19. Talal Asad, in *Formations of the Secular*, distinguishes between "'the secular' as an epistemic category and 'secularism' as a political doctrine" (1). He is thus able to contend, with regard to their relation: "If secularism as a doctrine requires the distinction between private reason and public principle, it also demands the placing of the 'religious' in the former by 'the secular'" (8). My discussion will not draw—at least not explicitly—on the precise distinction between the secular and secularism; it will use these two terms more or less interchangeably. (Nonetheless, as my aim is to understand how thought generates and functions under the aegis of the secular, it may be observed that my concern remains less with the "political doctrine" of secularism than with the "epistemic category" of the secular.) It will be become clear that I have various reservations about the ultimate viability of the secular. However, I will contend, most explicitly in the conclusion of chapter 5, that there is a certain quality associated with the secular (or secularism) that must be affirmed as such. In order to help distinguish this quality, as it is understood in itself, from the secular or secularism, I will make use of a terminological distinction between "the secular" (or "secularism) and "secularity" (where this latter term denotes the quality I want to affirm as such).

in which such a position becomes normative. In other words, it is a matter not just of asserting the dominance of a particular position—whether Christian or secular—but of involving this position within a broader plane of reality, such that the dominance of this particular position is mediated by its full congruence with the plane itself. What this requires, it should additionally be noted, is that particular positions that depart from the dominant particular position be understood as belonging, even if only implicitly, to the plane. The dominance of a particular position has sense only if there is a common plane of judgment between the dominant and the dominated. It is with regard to this construction of a plane—which, it must be observed, becomes transcendent to particular positions—that we can locate the fundamental continuity between Christian religion and the secular. There is, of course, a difference at the level of content—to call for a religious plane is certainly not to call for a secular plane! It should furthermore be admitted that this shift in content produces a difference in the way these planes operate. Nonetheless, before attending to this difference in the operation between the religious plane and the secular plane, it is important to emphasize what remains constant—namely, the installation of a transcendent plane that, in presenting itself as a universal aim, enables the hegemony of a particular position.

We have already seen how this is the case with Christianity, but the similarity of the case of the secular is witnessed to by Talal Asad's discussion of modernity, "in which secularism is centrally located."[20] According to Asad, those critics who point out that secular modernity does not name a coherent object are correct, but he adds that this non-objectivity points to a larger truth: if modernity does not appear objectively, this is not because it is not real, but rather because its reality is cast at a level prior to the emergence of discrete objects. It exists, to use the terminology I have been advancing, as a transcendent plane. Its adherents "*aim* at 'modernity,' and expect others (especially in the 'non-West') to do so too."[21] Secular modernity is aspirational, and this means that it is posed as the aspiration not only of those who explicitly adhere to it, but also of those who do not—indeed, it is as if the explicit adherents of secular modernity aspire to it on behalf of those who do not. This dynamic, it should be noted, bears a striking resemblance to the dynamic at the heart of the invention of religion, which subjected Christianity's others to the

20. Ibid., 12.
21. Ibid., 13. Emphasis in original.

aspiration of its own true incarnation of religion. At issue in each case is not the descriptive adequacy of a unitary aim; it is instead the production of this unitary aim on a level that transcends the data that are inadequately described by the aim. Asad echoes this point when he claims that the aspiration towards secular modernity "doesn't disappear when we simply point out that 'the West' isn't an integrated totality, that many people in the West contest secularism or interpret it in different ways, that the modern epoch in the West has witnessed many arguments and several irreconcilable aspirations. On the contrary, those who assume modernity *as a project* know that already."[22] What matters, in other words, is not the description of that which would exceed the unitary aim, but rather the projective inscription of this excess onto the transcendent plane, which has its own essential aim. It thus becomes clear that what exceeds the aim of the secular does not disrupt secular identity. On the contrary, it enables secular identity to operate in a more insidious register: the non-secular not only underwrites, by way of contrast or failure, secular identity, it also installs more deeply the need to invest in the secular as in a redemptive project. When the secular aspires on behalf of its others, then, it is also aspiring to become itself, for it is precisely by imagining its others as lacking the secular that it can give to itself its identifying project.

The isomorphism that I am observing between Christian religion and the secular makes it impossible to accept a narrative whereby the secular functions to emancipate us from Christianity or from religion as such. I have argued, for instance, that the Pauline concept of the world tends to refuse the immanent possibility of affirming worldliness, but this does not mean that another tendency, named as the secular, will necessarily succeed. In fact, the secular can be understood as remaining closer to Christian religion, in virtue of their common installation of a transcendent plane, than to any immanent affirmation of the world. One transcendent frame of the world has been rejected in favor of another. From a diasporic perspective, then, not much has changed, for the potentiality of interparticular relations, in which particularities immanently decompose and recompose one another without reference to a position of transcendence, remains precluded even when the secular project replaces the project of Christian religion. The secular, then, is not secular—how could it be, when it must interpret the significations of the vast majority of the world's inhabitants, those inhabitants that are religious, as so many privations of the secular?

22. Ibid.

How can the secular be worldly when it projects itself as something that lies above and beyond, and thus ahead, of the world as it is signified? To side with the secular, in short, is to judge, rather than to side with, the world. Gil Anidjar makes a similar point when he addresses the purported zero-sum opposition between secularism and religion. He contends that "to uphold *secularism* (or, for that matter, religion) as the key word for critical endeavors and projects today is, I am afraid, not to be that worldly. It is to oppose the world rather than that which makes and unmakes it as what it is not (or at least not yet). It is to oppose the world and those who inhabit it rather than those who make it unlivable."[23] Secularism, then, is not necessarily immanence, for immanence does not require that we choose between the signification of religion and the affirmation of the world. In fact, secularism is poorly understood as an immediate affirmation of the world, for it is, more basically, an injunction: to affirm the world, one must be against religious signification, since the true image of the world is one in which religious signification has been devalorized, or at least "resituated."[24]

This point is echoed by Asad's attention to the way in which the identification of the secular with the reality of the world is a construction, and one, more importantly perhaps—for what cannot be seen as a construction?—that emerges through a redrawing of boundaries. He notes, for instance, that although the secular's profanation of the purportedly religious sacred "appears to shift the gaze from the transcendental to the mundane, what it does is to re-arrange barriers between the illusory and the actual."[25] Secularism, in other words, is not something that seizes the world in order to liberate it from the constrictions of the transcendent; it is rather a discursive shift that disciplines us to recognize certain claims as fantastic and others as truthful. This is, in other words, to recognize the truth of the aspiration to be secular. Asad speaks, furthermore, of the way that the secular sets up a "duality" between "a world of self-authenticating things in which we *really* live as social beings and a religious world that exists only in our imagination."[26] Secularism, even though it

23. Anidjar, *Semites*, 50.

24. See Saba Mahmood's fascinating article, "Secularism, Hermeneutics, and Empire," 323–47, for an account of how this secular injunction is applied to Islam, whose "liberal reformers do not abandon the religious text but resituate it" (339).

25. Asad, *Formations of the Secular*, 36.

26. Ibid., 194.

claims to be a discourse about the world in itself, is unable to think the world apart from its own discourse; it makes the world in its own image. Accordingly, the claim that religious signification takes one away from the world is advanced not in the name of the world, but instead in the name of secularism.

Immanence, on the other hand, calls for a direct affirmation of the world, an affirmation that proceeds not by negating a dialectically opposed religious signification, but rather by a double affirmation—an affirmation, that is, of both the world as such, or the namelessness of immanence, *and* the signification that immanence necessarily produces. It may be argued, in response, that immanence is not far from the secular insofar as it, like the secular, claims that religious signification is fictive. Such a response, however, fails to see that, for immanence, the fictive character of religious signification is not something that is opposed to a supposedly authentic secular discourse on reality. (From the vantage of immanence, one of secularism's basic failures is its inability to recognize itself as yet another fictive signification.) Of course, it is important for immanence that one grasps signification as fictive, for otherwise one falls into transcendence by making one's own signification into the norm by which all other significations are rendered false. Nonetheless, to affirm the proper namelessness of immanence is not to have found the true, nameless name of reality; it is instead to realize that one necessarily produces fictive names for a reality that, as surplus, is fecund with regard to signification. There is, in short, no outside of fictive signification, and yet that is precisely what the secular claims to have found. All signification is fictive, and secularism falls short of this insight because it defines its identity in opposition to, and as the projective liberation from, something—i.e., religion—that is said to be caught up in the illusory, or the merely imaginative. We should, once again, discern echoes of Pauline thought in the logic of secularism: just as Christian religion superseded the material singularity—the difference—of non-Christian particularities, so secularism, with its unitary aim, supersedes the signification of its religious others.

The Transmutation of Religion

Yet if secularism can thus be understood as a repetition of Christian religion, wherein lies the separation? It is necessary to consider, without losing sight of this repetition, the way in which the secular is able to understand itself as a break with a Christian epoch. The absoluteness of such a break is questionable, due to the reasons mentioned above, as well as to the fact that the bounded space (geopolitically speaking) of Christian religion's "inside" is more or less identical to the bounded space of the secular's "inside." Despite all of this, there is a break, and so the task is to understand the nature of the break, but it is also to understand how this break does not disturb the hegemony of a certain European (or Euro-North American) bounded space but instead maintains it. Diaspora, of course, is fundamentally antagonistic towards any such bounded space. If we have seen how this antagonism is displayed against Christian religion, and how the same manner of antagonism applies to the secular's isomorphy with Christian religion, then now we must also see how it applies to what is novel in the secular.

Wherein lies the secular's break with Christian religion? It lies first of all in the shifting sense given to religion, which ceases to be that which is aimed at, and which is consummately found in Christianity, and instead becomes that which is to be surpassed. There was, it is well known, a concept of the secular prior to the emergence of what is now recognizable as secularism, but this previous secular was something internal to Christian religion—it did not, in other words, have any autonomy.[27] The dawn of secularism, on the other hand, is marked by the process through which the secular gains independence. It is by means of this process that the secular is able to refer to itself directly, such that it becomes, as Asad puts it, "self-authenticating," or perhaps more exactly that which is able to define the difference between the authentic and the fantastic. No longer positioned by Christian religion, the secular now positions both Christianity and religion. To put it quite simply: secularism constitutes itself by defining itself in opposition to religion, which is to say against Christian religion, but also, in the same moment, against what will come to be called—i.e., what secularism itself will define as—"world religions." Tomoko Masuzawa, in *The Invention of World Religions*, has provided an

27. As John Milbank, in *Theology and Social Theory*, has noted: "Once, there was no 'secular.' And the secular was not latent, waiting to fill more space with the steam of the 'purely human,' when the pressure of the sacred was relaxed. Instead there was the single community of Christendom. . . . The secular as a domain had to be instituted or *imagined*, both in theory and in practice" (9). Prior to this institution, the secular "was not a space, a domain, but a time—the interval between fall and *eschaton* where coercive justice, private property and impaired natural reason must make shift to cope with the unredeemed effects of sinful humanity" (9).

exemplary account of this shift. According to Masuzawa, "The modern discourse on religion and religions was from the beginning—that is to say, inherently, if also ironically—a discourse of secularization; at the same time, it was clearly a discourse of othering."[28] That is, the invention of something called world religions, along with the concomitant shift in the concept of religion, is part and parcel of the invention of the secular. This imbrication of secularization with the invention of world religions should not be perplexing, for the constitution of secular identity requires, as Masuzawa says, "a discourse of othering," and the other of secularism is religion. Of course, secularism has everything to do with European modernity, which is bound to the religion of Christianity. Accordingly, to become secular, Europe must emancipate itself from its own religious heritage, which means that it must re-imagine itself not as the confluence of the Hellenic and the Hebraic (the latter being non-"European"), but rather as the direct descendent of a Hellenism that had been tainted by the Hebraism of Christian religion.

Masuzawa notes that, with the emergence of secularism, one begins to encounter the idea "that, somehow, the *religious* heritage of European peoples was genealogically distinct and separate from all other aspects of their heritage. To put it simply, it suddenly appeared that Christianity could be at odds with the rest of what it meant to be European, rather than being its defining characteristic."[29] This is a notable shift from the epoch of Christian religion, in which Christianity was promoted as the midpoint or synthesis between its two rival religions, Judaism and Hellenism.[30] Secularism's discourse of world religions, on the contrary, pursues a Hellenizing purism, and this is articulated through the racist affirmation of the Aryan and negation of the Semitic.[31] If Europe is to be secular, then it must cease to be religious, and this means that it must cease to be Semitic. As Anidjar has insisted, the Semites "existed in European consciousness for precisely as long as Europe thought of itself as resolutely secular, as having achieved secularization. . . . As religion is said to wane

28. Masuzawa, *Invention of World Religions*, 20.

29. Ibid., 148.

30. Boyarin notes how certain "fourth-century Christian writers . . . readily accepted the notion that 'Hellenism' was a religion." He cites, for instance, Eusebius of Caeserea's assertion that Christianity is "that third form of religion midway between Judaism and Hellenism" (*Border Lines*, 205).

31. The categories of Aryan and Semitic were racializing from the beginning, though it should be noted that they were also presented as being properly "philological."

in the West, it is the East that emerges and becomes 'religion.'"[32] Note here the link between religion and race: those who are religious are those racially identified as the Semites, the others of the Aryans. This means that the Aryans, in order to be marked as secular, must be imagined as only accidentally tied to their Christian—i.e., Semitic—religion. What becomes apparent in this shift, Masuzawa observes, is that "what should be called 'uniquely universal' is not Christianity—a religion saddled with a complicated, compromised, and contested legacy—but instead, the Aryans."[33]

32. Anidjar, *Semites*, 20.

33. Masuzawa, *Invention of World Religions*, 206. The question of how, precisely, the discourse of race is engendered by and enables the functioning of secular modernity's understanding of itself, Christianity, and religion is one that, while certainly raised by my argument, is not fully addressed. For this I must make the (admittedly hackneyed) apology that a fully adequate treatment of this question—a treatment, I should add, that would have concomitantly needed to address the question of the biopolitical—remains outside of the scope of this book. Still, the problematic remains. J. Kameron Carter's book, *Race*, offers a compelling account of the way in which the dawn of modernity brought into being a Christianity that was identified with whiteness. His book is impressively thorough, and makes an argument that I support. The question that my argument poses, however, can be seen as somewhat complementary to his aims. What I would query, specifically, is the way in which Carter appears to locate the failure of Christian thinking primarily with the dawn of the modern, such that it would remain possible to imagine Christianity, prior to the colonial endeavor, as a positive point of reference. The difficulty with such a possibility—though it must be said that it is in fact a *possibility* left in place by Carter, rather than a thesis he explicitly advances—is that it does not address the way in which the emergence of Christian identity in Pauline and patristic thought already set in motion tendencies that would make possible a dominative or hierarchical conception of Christianity. The problematic I am trying to articulate is perhaps most evident in Christianity's relationship to Judaism, or to the material singularity of Jewish existence. As I have argued, the invention of Christian religion (which, of course, occurs well before secular modernity) takes place in such a manner that this material singularity is figured in terms of lack. While such lack is not understood in terms of race (at least not in the sense of modern racism), it remains important to interrogate the relationship between the Christian figuration of Jewish flesh as lacking the perfection of the spirit—a figuration, I have observed, that is already present in Pauline thought—and the distinctively modern figuration of racism, which obviously emerges specifically in virtue of anti-Semitism. The need for such interrogation is made especially prominent by Carter's attention to the way in which an affirmation of Jesus's "Jewish flesh" (30) serves to antagonize racializing discourse. How, it might be asked, should we understand the relationship between a Christian logic that defines itself in terms of Jesus's Jewish flesh and a Christian logic that has thought Jewish flesh in general—the flesh that Jesus shares with Jews who do not understand him as "the Christ," with those who affirm the flesh that Christianity, in order to define itself as such, dialectically defines itself *against*—in terms of an allegory of the spirit? Carter has indicated to me that the book he is currently working on already aims to take up the sort of questions I am here presenting—it will do so, in fact, precisely by looking at the formulations of Christology in early Christianity.

The concept of religion thus functions in tandem with the discourse of race, and yet the latter has tended to become concealed by the former. To bring race out of its concealment under the cover of religion is to call into question the adequacy of seeing the tension between Christianity and secularism as the primary opposition. What becomes far more convincing is the possibility of understanding this tension as a relatively minor squabble that occurs against the background of a presupposed, or perhaps internalized, Christian-secular racism. Thus Pope Benedict XVI, who sees the rise of secularism as an unhappy obstacle blocking the path of a Christianized world, claims that "it is not surprising that Christianity, despite its origins and some significant developments in the East, finally took on its historically decisive character in Europe."[34] It is as if he is assuring his audience that, despite the claims of secularism, it is not necessary to choose between Christianity and Europe. Yes, he admits, Christianity's "origins" were in "the East," and there were undoubtedly "some significant developments" that took place outside of Europe. But these are not essential, for what really matters is that Christianity became "historically decisive" when it became European (and this, he adds, was no contingent occurrence—the becoming-European of Christianity was an "intrinsic necessity").[35] Against secularism, then, Christianity is advocated, but it is a Christianity that conforms to the normative Aryanism of secularism's opposition to the Semitic East. Christian religion, as imagined by the Catholicism of Benedict, may oppose secularism, but in doing so it does not yet begin to oppose racism.

Similarly, the Protestantism of Barth fails to make much headway in opposing the territorial dominance of Europe. Barth, in fact, remains in league with secularism above all through his thoroughgoing critique of religion, which he says is merely "human manufacture." Importantly, this claim about religion is universal, which is to say it applies to each and every religion, to Christianity just as much as to the so-called world religions. Nonetheless, this does not mean the end of Christian dominance, for if religion is understood as "human manufacture," it appears as such in contrast to divine revelation. Religion, he says, is "the attempted replacement of the divine work by a human manufacture. The divine reality offered and manifested to us in revelation is replaced by a concept of

34. Benedict XVI, "Papal Address at University of Regensburg."

35. Ibid. Indeed, Benedict speaks not only of an "intrinsic necessity of a rapprochement between Biblical faith and Greek inquiry," he also asserts that the "encounter between the Biblical message and Greek thought did not happen by chance."

God arbitrarily and willfully evolved by man."[36] All religion fails, then, but one detects a certain primacy of Christianity among the failed religions: each and every religion will fall short of the divine, but Christianity, even as it includes itself among this group of failures, is able to exclude itself; it is in Christianity, after all, that one encounters the event, or the revelation, against which religion appears as failure. Christian religion is like all other religions, and yet it is also absolutely unlike all other religions, for only through Christianity does one encounter the revelation that manifests divine reality. It will be said that the revelation of God must be distinguished from the religion of Christianity; yet it must also be said in response that the very distinction between divine revelation and human religion is produced *by* Christianity.

Perhaps to take this distinction seriously is to give up on Christianity, and to give up on religion—perhaps, in other words, it is to enter into secularism. Of course, this would not be pure secularism, insofar as it proclaims the revelation of divine reality. What I contend, however, is that this difference on the point of revelation is a minor difference that obscures a broader agreement on two points: first, that religion is something to be superseded; second, that this task of supersession, no matter whether it comes from revelation (Barth) or Europe (secularism), is one that allows a distinction to be made between the West and its "religious" others.[37] This broader concord amidst minor disagreement can be seen by comparing Barth to Hegel: whereas Hegel envisioned the supersession, or at least the "Aufhebung," of other religions by Christianity, and then of Christianity by a secularized "Spirit," Barth calls for the "Aufhebung" of religion by revelation. Even as they disagree on the direction in which sublation should move, they both agree that it should move away from religion. Furthermore, they agree that in this moving away from religion Christianity gains pride of place—it is subject to the universal critique of religion, yet it is also the means by which one is able to make this critique

36. Barth, *Church Dogmatics* I/2, 302.

37. Toscano (*Fanaticism*, 207) cites Barth's equation (in *Church and the Political Problem*, 43) of Islam with Nazism: "Karl Barth declared that it was 'impossible to understand National Socialism unless we see it in fact as a *new Islam*, its myth as a new Allah, and Hitler as this new Allah's prophet.'" Barth's equation is especially important to keep in mind insofar as his opposition to Nazism is sometimes used to valorize his theology. What such an equation indicates, however, is that Barth's opposition to Nazism's intra-European Orientalism did not escape extra-European Orientalism. For accounts of the connection between internalized and externalized modalities of Orientalism, see Hess, *Germans, Jews, and the Claims of Modernity*; and Anidjar, *The Jew, the Arab*.

and thus surpass religion. For Barth, just as for Benedict, Christian opposition to secularism proceeds only by first accepting the terms of secularism: for Benedict, there was a conformity to secularism's Aryan ideology, its commitment to European supremacy; for Barth, there is conformity to secularism's peculiar criticism of religion, whereby the universal opposition to religion conceals and thus leaves in place a distinction between Christianity (or post-Christianity) and world religions, a distinction that enables Christian supremacy.

This Christian opposition to secularism, as it is set forth by the representative Catholic and Protestant figures of Benedict and Barth, witnesses to the fact that there is a genuine difference between Christianity and secularism. At the same time, it witnesses equally to the fact that such opposition does not extend to the mode of dominance—it is not, in other words, an anti-secularism that proceeds in the name of diaspora. Christian religion is displaced by the binary of the secular and religion. Hidden in this break, however, is an abiding territorial dominance: Christian dominance is displaced by the dominance of European modernity, but the place remains the same, it is the same bounded space. Also hidden in this break is a certain equivocation with regard to the concept of religion—indeed, it is precisely this equivocation, which we can already glimpse (though from a Christian perspective) in Barth's critique of religion, that enables the continuation of territorial dominance. The equivocation lies in the fact that the difference between Christian religion and world religions is concealed. Secularism criticizes religion as such, but note the way in which this critique functions: it is posed against Christian religion, yet it is thusly posed only insofar as it is likewise—and perhaps initially—posed against the non-West, those others of Europe. At a formal level, then, secularism is consistent—it does not contradict itself—but this consistency enables a differential between the West and the non-West. The secular West rejects religion for itself, but it does so, one might say, as the price that must be paid in order to reject the non-West by characterizing this non-West as religious. The West comes out ahead, not because it is has no religious stain, but because it knows how to overcome—either through outright rejection or sublation—this religious stain by being secular, whereas the non-West lacks such knowledge. Again, what we find in secularism is a supersessionist discourse, just as we found in Christian religion. This is to say that even as a real break emerges between Christian religion and secularism, the mode of domination, and the construction of a hegemonic "bounded space," remains constant.

Returning, then, to the equivocation of religion at the heart of the invention of the secular, we can say that the critique of religion has a double valence. There is, first, the religion that is found in the other, which is so essential to the other that the other cannot but be religious. It is here, in fact, that one can see the logic by which the West connects discourse on world religions to racial discourse. Second, however, there is the religion that is found in the West, the religion that is superseded by secularism. One might say that it is precisely through the religion of the West, i.e., Christian religion, that the secular becomes possible. According to this interpretation, Christianity is differentiated from other religions insofar as it is always already secular; it is the acorn that carries in itself the teleological aim of secularism's oak tree. Yet even if this notion of Christianity as secularism *avant le lettre* is disavowed, such that one sees secularism as something that revolts against rather than reforms Christianity, the effect remains the same: the subjectivity of secularism remains linked to the subjectivity of Christianity. The endgame, in either case, is that the concept of religion functions equivocally when it is applied to Christianity as well as to non-Christian religions. And it is precisely this equivocation that enables secularism to function—just as Christian religion functioned—to the benefit of a dominant bounded space.

Is this not, Anidjar asks, the continuation of Christianity by other means? Noting the connection between religion and race, he remarks: "Like that unmarked race, which, in the related discourse of racism, became invisible or 'white,' Christianity invented the distinction between religious and secular, and thus it *made* religion. It made religion the problem—rather than itself."[38] Religion, I have argued, emerged through Christianity's auto-identification, and so it would be incorrect to say that religion begins only with secularism. Nonetheless, what Anidjar rightly observes is what I would recast as a transmutation in the concept of religion, a shift from something that is allied with the Christian to something that is opposed to the secular. Does this mean that there is a common subject beneath this shift, a subject that was once religious, and then secular, but always dominant? Anidjar contends that "secularism is a name Christianity gave itself when it invented 'religion,' named its other or others as 'religions.'"[39] Secularism is the modality by which Christianity both erases and maintains itself as normative. According to this narrative, Christianity immunized

38. Anidjar, *Semites*, 47.
39. Ibid., 48.

itself from critique by changing its name, by re-inventing itself as secularism, a re-invention that required religion to be seen as object of critique. This narrative is largely compelling, but it is not without its difficulties. If it is the case (as I take it to be) that the concept of religion is something that predates the invention of the secular, then it will be necessary to speak not of a secular invention of religion, but rather of a secular transmutation of religion. This transmutation would be one whereby religion ceases to be something that allows Christianity's supersession of its others and instead becomes something that allows secularism's supersession of its others. There is, no doubt, a common bounded space, and a corresponding subject, running beneath these supersessions, but how should we characterize this commonality or this subject? It begins by being religious, but it continues by eschewing religion. Accordingly, the subject of dominance must be understood at a point prior to the distinction between religion and non-religion. This is also to say that it will be insufficient simply to assert that this subject is Christianity, for even if this subject maintains the territorial dominance effected by Christianity, it does in some meaningful sense break with Christianity when it becomes secular. A discourse of antagonism is absolutely necessary here, but such a discourse begins by conceiving its enemy—and this enemy cannot only be Christianity secularized (though it is that as well), it must also (and more fundamentally) be that which enables such things as Christianity and secularism, and such mutations as the one that takes place in religion when Christianity is superseded by secularism. What is necessary, in other words, is to address the mode of relation *between* Christianity, religion, and secularism.

Differential Antagonism

It is exigent to construct a discourse that is antagonistic towards a certain mode of dominance, and the thesis here being propounded is that this mode of dominance deploys itself differentially. This means it will be insufficient to name the mode of dominance as Christianity, or even as Christianity secularized. It will furthermore be insufficient to make religion, or its apparent inescapability, into the enemy. If we are to conceive the mode of dominance, then it will be necessary to see it not as one of three terms, nor as the manner in which one term makes use of the others, but instead as the differential relations of these three terms. The mode of dominance does not, of course, reside somehow beyond or behind these three terms, but neither does it identify itself with one of them. As it does not exist outside these terms, it would be more precise to say that it is the effect of their relations, or that it exists precisely as the set of relations that emerge through the differences of Christianity/religion, secularism/ Christianity, and secularism/religion. These differences condition one another in a circular manner, such that each difference establishes itself against the background of the others. This makes an antagonistic discourse more difficult—indeed, it may very well be the ability of the mode of dominance to hide behind its differentiated terms that makes it so hard to pin down. If you are against Christian dominance, then you must be for secularism, which manages to maintain the dominance deployed by Christianity. If you are then against secularism, are you consequently for religion? If so, how is one for religion if Christianity remains, in the background, the epitome of religion? And what would it mean to affirm religion when its invention is linked to Christianity but its transmutation is bound up in secularism?

Any attempt to evade dominance by valorizing one of the differentiated terms will fail, and this is because dominance is established through differentiation itself. Accordingly, any antagonism wishing to become adequate to the dominance it opposes will have to be a discourse of difference. This does not mean it should seek either to straightforwardly oppose or affirm difference: one cannot oppose difference, for difference is always already at work; neither does it suffice to affirm difference brutely (to affirm it apart from the contexts in which it is deployed). What matters is to understand how difference is enacted by the mode of domination, and to conceive how difference might be differently enacted by an alternative modality. This is at once an a priori operation of theory and an a posteriori operation of genealogy. I have sought to provide the latter by tracking, in this and the previous chapters, the emergence of the hegemonic discursive regimes of Pauline thought, Christian religion, and the secular; the former, I am arguing, can be found in a theory of diasporic immanence. The peculiar advantage of diaspora is, in fact, that it articulates itself at the level of difference. Diasporic thought is necessarily in-between; it concerns itself neither with this nor with that, but rather with the difference between this and that. It seeks to inhabit and think the difference directly, and to compose new relations from differential tensions. In other words, diaspora is able to conceive, stand against, and move beyond the mode of domination because it is just as differential as such domination. This means that if we speak of a diasporic excess, it is not the excess of one term to another, not the mere excess of an inassimilable remainder—it is, more fundamentally, the excess of difference as such to its deployment and expression in the mode of domination.

Difference, however, is always expressed, which is to say that it is not enough simply to proclaim the merits of difference, meritorious though it may be. More than this, what is necessary is to imagine how the terms differentiated by the mode of dominance might be decomposed—how they might be delinked from the relations they bear to one another, and thus from the meanings they carry—as well as how they might enter into new relations. This is what diaspora seeks to imagine. Diaspora therefore is both antagonistic and constructive: antagonistic insofar as it aims to conceive difference prior to its resolution into a distinction between dominating and dominated terms; constructive insofar as it seeks not to move beyond signifying terms, as if they could be erased, but rather to construct new, non-dominative relations between them. Diaspora does not belong to an eternity untouched by dominant significations, for this would render it transcendent. It does, however, belong to an immanent surplus, a surplus that, although coded by the signifying relations of a mode of dominance, can never finally be reduced to these relations. Diaspora is thus the liberation of surplus from the domination of Christianity, religion, and secularism, yet this liberation must itself be effected by a re-expression of what is expressed by these terms. The line of antagonism is to be drawn not between one of these terms and its others, or between all of these terms and something that would transcend them, but instead between an immanent, diasporic conception of these terms and their deployment by a mode of dominance.

The Differentiality of Differentialities

With Beginning, _____ created *Elohim* (Gen 1:1)

—*Zohar*[1]

Affliction and Mimesis

IF IT IS TRUE, as I am proposing, that life has been significantly afflicted by the logics at work in Christianity, religion, and secularism, or by the mode of dominance deployed through and as their differentials, then what would it mean to be cured of this affliction? The task of addressing such a question becomes particularly exigent when the possibility of a transcendent cure—a cure that would reveal something above and beyond, and thus untouched by, these names—is refused. It is not a matter, once and for all, of getting Christianity, or religion, or secularism, "right," as if a purified version of one of these terms would provide resolution. A transcendent cure must fail, for it remains incapable of responding to the differential nature of the affliction. Nonetheless, the impossibility of a transcendent cure does not, in and of itself, provide an alternative cure. If anything, awareness of this impossibility serves to intensify the demand to construct an alternative cure—after all, it is precisely the difficulty, or even apparent unavailability, of an alternative cure that amplifies

---

1. *Zohar*, 50.

the temptation to seek a cure unaffected by our affliction. Is there not, in other words, a certain positive feedback loop between the impossibility of a transcendent cure and the desire for such a cure? Indeed, even to point to such a compulsion to repeat transcendence risks inscribing itself further into this positive feedback loop. We must therefore advance from critique of the temptation towards transcendence to construction of an immanent cure.

What is required is the capacity to imagine a cure that would be mimetic in character. A mimetic cure is one in which the source of affliction enters into the cure—or, to put it otherwise, one in which the cure stems from exposure to the affliction. It is this last point that fundamentally distinguishes the immanent from the transcendent cure, for the latter insists that healing begins by renouncing affliction, by imagining and committing oneself to a future that will never have been determined by the source of what engenders sickness. From the perspective of an immanent cure, on the other hand, such transcendence appears as a fantasy, and a fantasy that functions to conceal the very nature of the affliction. It is not just that it fails to heal, it is also that its failure to heal actually misdirects attention—that is, it directs attention from the source of affliction. Let me make clear, however, that to oppose the desire to transcend sickness is not simply to affirm sickness. A mimetic cure is not a resigned exposure to affliction, but rather a re-staging of such exposure. It is, more precisely, a re-staging that would decompose the elements that afflict in order to recompose them in the name of health. While such a re-staging brings about an immanent relation between sickness and cure, it also brings about the potentiality for new relations. If the affliction is relational, then the cure, insofar as it is also relational, may enter into immanence with what afflicts without thereby remaining subject to affliction—for the relations may become altered.

What is at work here is the connection between interpellative determination and the excess of immanent surplus. There is no escaping the inherited significations, the names by which we have been called, yet the inescapability of signification is not equivalent to the inescapability of affliction. In fact, it is the tendency to disavow interpellative signification that leads us to turn away from what causes affliction, and thus from what might cure us of such affliction. The spell of signification is only deepened by the desire to transcend the afflictive significations in virtue of separate healing significations. Indeed, is this not what

Christianity did with regard to Rome, and what secularism did with regard to Christianity? Another effort along these lines—a transcendence of Christianity, secularism, and religion—is not promising. A new mode of healing is preferable, and such a mode involves no leap out of affliction, but instead a certain re-staging of affliction. We are inescapably interpellated by our affliction, our life is immanent to signification, but there is likewise an immanent surplus. To think our immanence to affliction is to disengage this surplus from the signifying relations that make us suffer; it is to use the namelessness of immanence as a curative agent, one that does not bring us beyond names, but that does allow us to construct new relations between them. This construction of novel relations, of newly mixed names, is the operation of diaspora.

Obviously, in order for a cure to be effective, it must have priority over the sickness it heals. What is not obvious, however, is that this priority needs to be understood in terms of chronology—whereby the cure lies in restoring an original essence that has been historically corrupted—or of transcendence—whereby the cure lies in a realm of being that is ultimately unaffected by the elements that afflict. The priority of diaspora lies elsewhere, namely in that which it constructs, and this is possible because it draws on a surplus that is immanent to and deployed by the affliction, but that is likewise irreducible to the afflictive relations. Transcendence will have been prior from the origin, whether historical or ontological, whereas diasporic immanence achieves its priority through constructing something in the wake of afflictive relations. In this sense, though diaspora is always second with respect to signification, it bears the capacity to construct beginnings—beginnings that lie not in their restoration of origins or their incarnation of the transcendent, but solely in themselves.

Contingent Potentiality and Discursive Tradition

Diasporic thought stands in the wake of something it will not have determined, but this stance is simultaneously one of resistance. It is able to exceed that in relation to which it appears as second, but its ability to do so hinges on its ability to think, in a decompositional manner, what has already historically emerged—what presents itself as initially established. My account has traced the course of this historical establishment from Christian religion to secularism; a decomposition of this established trajectory can therefore benefit from rethinking the establishment of

Christianity. Furthermore, if it is the case, as I have argued, that the establishment of Christianity occurs in conjunction with the establishment of religion, and that the establishment of religion is likewise involved in the establishment of a substantive difference between Christianity and Judaism, then it would be apt for a rethinking of the establishment of Christianity to commence with a rethinking of the establishment of Christian-Jewish difference. It is with this aim in mind that I now turn to Yoder's account of the Jewish-Christian schism.

There are many perspectives from which this account may be evaluated, and the most obvious of these is that of the Christian tradition. However, it is worth considering that such a perspective may run up against certain limits in assessing the import of Yoder's account. To say this, of course, is to risk valorizing—against my intention—a secular perspective that would claim to have transcended the purportedly limited vantages of a particular religious tradition. Despite this hazard, it is important to maintain the consideration, for Yoder's account calls into question the emergence of this tradition, at least insofar as it discretely exists. Specifically, what Yoder's account implies is that the "schism" between— or the partition of—Judaism and Christianity should not be taken as a necessity. It is, in fact, with regard to this specific event that Yoder unfolds some more generic ruminations on the role of contingency and historical development. He puts it quite directly when he asserts, "It did not have to be."[2] This, he says, is the "historian's axiom": it functions as the condition of possibility for the telling of history; only if what happened did not have to happen can there emerge the void in understanding that is filled in by the historian. Yet once this is admitted, something else becomes apparent, which is that the axiom of the historian also calls into question every product of the historian. This is because history-telling, even if it begins by presuming the openness of contingency, cuts off this selfsame contingency through the explanation it provides. History-telling thus locks us into a rather vicious circularity: in order to make sense of what happened, one commits oneself to imagining what happened in terms of necessity, yet the need for explanation points to a contingency that remains irreducible to the necessity expressed in history-telling.

To stand against historical necessity is thus to affirm contingency and potentiality. Indeed, what is striking about Yoder's insistence on such contingency and potentiality is its reliance on something akin to an ontology

2. Yoder, *Jewish-Christian Schism Revisited*, 43.

of force. The "perspective on what *could have been* is not 'realistic' in the sense of positivism; it refuses to let 'the way things are' have the last word. It is, however, realistic in a *deeper* sense. It pushes us to ask far more ambitious and complex questions about all of the forces which were at work, and about how things could have been otherwise. . . . It drives us to take stock carefully of the powers and resources which were there but were not tapped, or which were at work but did not win out."[3] This passage is much more than a pious statement recommending a degree of openness with regard to the past. It is more fundamentally a claim about "reality," namely that such reality is genuinely missed if we take our cues from what is historically established. There is, in other words, a "deeper" reality out of which history becomes established, a reality to which we must attend if we are to properly contextualize what becomes historically dominant. Furthermore, this deeper reality is not at all transcendent; it is closer to an immanent context, composed as it is of "forces" and "powers" that, though unselected, were present in the same manner as those that were selected. To put Yoder's point in the terminology I have been using, these forces are a differential milieu out of which forms of identity emerge. Such forms are effective, of course, but this does not mean that their effectiveness exhausts reality; they deploy yet remain irreducible to an immanent surplus. There are, in other words, powers that bear witness ontologically to a series of events that "could have been otherwise." If we fail to attend to these powers, then we miss contingency, a contingency that belongs not to an epistemological abstraction but rather to the depth of the real, the complexity of which bears the potentiality for what would be "otherwise."

What must be emphasized here is the generic sense of Yoder's remarks. They are occasioned by his reflections on the Jewish-Christian schism, but they are clearly set forth as principles whose scope extends well beyond this specific event. Accordingly, it would be insufficient to see in these remarks a straightforwardly "Christian" theory of reality. On the contrary, the theory of reality to which they witness must be applied just as much to the establishment of Christianity as to all other historically established forms. Even if we identify Yoder's thought with Christianity,

3. Ibid., 44. It should be noted that "the powers" that Yoder here has in mind are not to be identified with "the Powers," mentioned in chapter 3, that functioned to structure or determine an unredeemed existence. What Yoder here means by "powers" has to do with something productive, it has to do with the reality of alternative possibilities, rather than with an already determined structuration of what is possible. I mark this difference in definition by either capitalizing or not capitalizing the word.

strict adherence to this thought calls into question the viability of the identification of something called Christianity. This is true not only in terms of
the generic sense of Yoder's account, but also when looked at through the
more specific event of the Jewish-Christian schism to which Yoder applies
his generic claims. There did not have to be, he contends, a parting of the
ways. Since the identifiable realities conceived as Judaism and Christianity
are inextricable from this partition, it follows that they too are unnecessary. Whatever it is to which Yoder is seeking to become adequate, then,
it cannot be Christianity, for Christianity is an effect of the partition that
Yoder is rendering unnecessary. The deeper reality in which contingency
and potentiality are implicated is not the effect of an essentially Christian
thought; it is actually closer to the aim of Yoder's account to observe that
adherence to a Christian essence risks obscuring this deeper reality.

It is often observed that Yoder is a radical opponent of Christendom,
which is obviously an exemplary embodiment of what I have critically
construed as Christian religion—but it is not entirely obvious how we are
to understand the nature of Yoder's opposition. Does it proceed in virtue
of a purer or truer or more authentic Christianity, such that Christendom
is seen as a corruption of the original Christian essence? There are certainly grounds for this interpretation. But how would such an interpretation address the emphasis here granted by Yoder to that depth of reality
that sets forth a contingency and potentiality in excess of what is historically established? What I am suggesting is that the condition of possibility for Yoder's critique of Christendom, or of Christian religion, should
not be conceived in terms of an essential Christianity. This is because the
desire for an essential Christianity would be inscribed within the actually
existing Christianity constituted by the sort of history-telling that Yoder
opposes. A critique of Christendom in the name of an ideal Christian essence does not get to the core difficulty. The difficulty is not that actually
existing Christianity fails to conform to ideal Christianity; it resides, prior
to this distinction between actually existing and ideal, in the constitution
of an identifiable Christianity. This, I am claiming, is the implication of
Yoder's critique of history-telling, and thus it is here, rather than in an
ideal Christianity, that we should locate the condition of possibility for
his critique of Christendom.

It should be made clear, however, that this is not to claim that
Yoder's critique is generated by a vantage that is somehow strictly beyond
Christianity. This is manifestly not the case, for Yoder's work is marked by

his insistence on maintaining fidelity to Jesus, and on rigorously thinking through the consequences of such fidelity. When, for instance, he opposes history-telling that would make war inevitable, he does so not simply in the name of contingency's irreducibility to necessity, but just as much—if not more so—in the name of Jesus's renunciation of violence. Indeed, the critique of history-telling that I am citing unfolds in relation to his commitment to a perspective that would be more "repentant."[4] As much as some might be tempted to see in this an invocation of a universal and neutralizing call to conscience, it requires an act of substantive hermeneutical violence to rest in this evaluation. When Yoder speaks of the imperative of repentance, it is a repentance shaped by a discourse that takes Jesus's call to repent and believe as central. Thus, while I am claiming that Yoder's critical re-evaluation of the "historian's axiom" most certainly commits him to his own axiom of contingency and potentiality, I would also claim that it is just as much the case that this critique unfolds in virtue of his commitment to the axiom that history-telling falls short when it does not proceed by means of cross and resurrection.[5] This is to say that Yoder's critical capacities proceed from a Christian vantage, even as they call for a vantage that would subject the purely Christian vantage to critique.

Is this a contradiction? It would certainly appear so as long as one maintains a supersessionist logic—one that would require us to assent either to a Christian supersession of the "secular" vantage or to a "secular" supersession of the Christian vantage. But why must one accept this binary? After all, if we attend to the specific context of Yoder's critique of history-telling—namely the non-necessity of the Jewish-Christian schism—we will find him explicitly asserting: "*Tertium datur.*"[6] His claim that a third choice is possible is one that can be similarly applied in order to deny that his critique must be *either* without *or* within Christianity. Even the affirmation of *tertium datur* is simultaneously without and within: it stems from a theory about history-telling as such, but also from the need to imagine that "God's purpose might have been to offer a different future from the one which actually came to be."[7] There is no need

4. Ibid., 43.

5. See, for instance, Yoder's claim that: "The relationship between the obedience of God's people and the triumph of God's cause is not a relationship of cause and effect but one of cross and resurrection." *Politics of Jesus*, 232.

6. Yoder, *Jewish-Christian Schism Revisited*, 51. Emphasis in original.

7. Ibid., 47.

to choose between purely ontological discourse about reality in a deeper sense and theological discourse about God's purpose. Yet, precisely because of this non-necessity, it is incumbent upon us to oppose both the idea that God's purpose is mere code for the depth of reality and the idea that the depth of reality is mere code for God's purpose. Yoder, I am claiming, echoes in his own manner Spinoza's proposal that being should be called "God, or Nature."

The act of placing the discursive tradition of Christianity under critique and the act of maintaining fidelity to something that is marked by Christian signification are therefore not mutually exclusive. They become mutually exclusive only insofar as it is imagined that one discursive tradition must be opposed to another, and yet it is precisely this mutual exclusion of discursive traditions that diaspora refuses. It makes this refusal, once again, in a double sense: insofar as it recognizes the fundamental impropriety of every attempt to name a properly nameless immanence, it refuses to reduce reality to Christian signification that would transcend all non-Christian significations of reality; insofar as it recognizes that immanence's surplus requires the production of signification, it refuses to see Christian signification as a too-particular occlusion of a reality that transcends all signification. The former error, present in the paradigms of TP and TO, is central to the establishment of Christian religion, whereas the latter error, present in the paradigms of PD and PE, is central to the establishment of secularism. My argument is not necessarily that Yoder has explicitly articulated and committed himself to the exact theory of diaspora I am here articulating, but, more precisely, that his thought may be usefully understood as an indication of such a theory. By turning to Yoder, in other words, we are able to indicate how diaspora can make sense of and call for an intrinsically differential style of thinking—one that does not submit to the binarized differences that make possible the mode of domination that we all too easily encounter when we begin to think about Christianity, secularism, and religion. The logic of *tertium non datur* is what allows the domination (or supersession) of one term over the other, and as long as we accept this logic we fail to accede to the possibilities of differential composition that would mimetically re-enact these terms through the construction of non-dominative relations. If this sort of mimetic re-enactment is necessary for a cure, then Yoder's thought helps us move in a more redemptive direction.

The Differentiality of Differentialities:
Christianity and Judaism

My thesis that the choice between imagining oneself as either within or without Christianity is a false one may be further developed by the adjacent thesis that Christianity is inconsistent from the beginning. It is not that later events have led us to the judgment that the discursive tradition of Christianity should be abandoned or even qualified from the outside; it is rather that the discursive tradition of Christianity was never "one" in the first place. This was implied by my earlier account of the intrinsically differential nature of Christian declaration, which calls for the decomposition of identitarian forms and the composition of new relations. Importantly, these new relations should not be understood as generating yet another form of identity, one perhaps that would transcend all previous identities. Indeed, it is exactly the tendency towards a transcendent identity that I have espied and criticized in Pauline thought. If these relations are new, it is not because their identity is novel, but rather because the character of relationality is novel; the difference that matters lies not between two kinds of identity, but between the identitarian and the differential. If Christianity is thusly understood, then any identifiably Christian discourse is relativized.[8] Of course, the emergence of a Christian discursive tradition is not ultimately avoidable, nor is it necessarily a failure—a declaration is already signification, any attempt to affirm this declaration involves signification, and there is nothing intrinsically "fallen" about signification. Nonetheless, it is one thing to imagine Christian signification as a creative and differential operation, and another thing entirely to imagine Christian signification as forming an internally coherent, or auto-referential, discourse that provides a transcendent vantage on the potentiality of contingent encounters. Diaspora, because it calls for the composition of novel differential relations, can stand with contingent potentiality against any identitarian Christian discourse; it can do so, furthermore, without having to straightforwardly refuse Christian signification, since it is possible to see, in the declaration repeated by this signification, an affirmation of a potentiality that exceeds Christian identity. This has nothing to do with the assertion of a pure Christian identity, an

8. This relativization, it should be noted, is enjoined not, as a certain Barthian trajectory would have it, by the tension between the divine word (Jesus who is named Christ) and human words, but instead by the tension between the declaration of differential possibility and the tendency of any discursive tradition to sediment into an identity.

essence from which Christian signification has fallen, and everything to do with a differentiality at the heart of what will be called Christianity—a differentiality that, if affirmed, must render its affirmer both within and without any ensuing Christian discourse. Christian declaration was differential from the very beginning, and so to begin with it is always to begin again, to undertake a differential repetition of a differential.

Does this mean diaspora, by affirming what is differential, calls for the end of all discursive tradition? Not entirely. What it demands is that discursive traditions become capable of existing differentially, which is to say of becoming diasporic. In other words, it would be inadequate to create a new binary between discursive tradition and diaspora. Diaspora is not a discursive tradition, but rather a differential dynamic that enables discursive traditions to exceed themselves—it is, in fact, the condition of possibility for the construction of a discursive tradition. I have sought to make this point with regard to the discursive tradition of Christianity: it is not a matter of being for or against, within or without, this discourse; one can be within it only insofar as one is able to be without it. I should hasten to add that this is not some "special" characteristic of Christianity. My thesis is instead that the double character of signification, whereby it is both excessively improper and necessary, renders it capable of producing names as well as of undermining names through the production of new names. Under these conditions, any discursive tradition will be both a novel construction and something that exceeds itself. If it is unable to affirm this excess, it will either sediment into a transcendent identity or create a context in which its supersession, often by yet another identity, becomes difficult to avoid.

Yet it is important, having made these remarks, to offer a critical qualification of Yoder's account of diaspora (which influences, but must not be conflated with, the account of diaspora I have been advancing).[9] Boyarin, amidst a generally appreciative response to Yoder's discussion of the partition of Judaism and Christianity—one that goes so far as to say that "Yoder, I think, truly and successfully supersedes supersessionism"— makes what I take to be a crucially important criticism, namely that Yoder's use of diaspora ends up engendering an essentialist account of Judaism.[10] Obviously, diaspora can function positively as a predicate common to both Christianity (as Yoder advances it) and Judaism (as Boyarin advances it),

9. Yoder advances the notion of diaspora as a constructive alternative to "schism."

10. Boyarin, "Judaism as a Free Church," 9.

and in this way it can provide a means of approach beyond partition. The difficulty, however, is that such an approach simultaneously risks repeating the founding gesture of Christianity, which is to make its conception of itself normative for other religions' conceptions of themselves. The essence of Christianity interpellates its religious others—and even if this essence is conceived in terms of diaspora, which is to say with a tendency towards pluralism, this tendency is cut short insofar as the essence continues to be imposed on the religious other. "This is a tricky moment," Boyarin says, "because, after all, it is precisely . . . diasporism to which I have been in my work and political life calling Jews, Jewry, and Judaism as well. However, I have been trying to be careful—I hope—in not defining an *essence* to Judaism, while Yoder is, I think, not careful enough."[11]

The point I wish to add is that Boyarin's remark cuts against diaspora as a Christian possession, but not against the logic of diaspora itself (at least not as I seek to articulate it). This distinction can be made insofar as we observe that the inconsistency affirmed by diaspora, as the condition enabling the constitution of differential bonds, is not just something that runs between discursive traditions; it is also something that runs within discursive traditions.[12] In other words, to affirm diaspora is not to affirm an idea to which a plurality of discursive traditions must submit, for this would be to make diaspora transcendent and thus to lose the very differences between discursive traditions that condition it—indeed, this comes dangerously close to a theory of diaspora as analogical participation. If diaspora is to be enacted between discursive traditions, in their inconsistency with regard to one another, then it must first become capable of submitting to the specific inconsistencies within such traditions. Diaspora

11. Ibid., 13.

12. In speaking here (and in what follows) of "inconsistency," what I have in mind is the sense that Eric Santner gives to the term in *On the Psychotheology of Everyday Life*, 102. When considering the "enigmatic messages" that are given by "the symbolic tradition and order into which one is born," he makes clear that "inconsistency is something different from incompleteness, from a reference to a lack that could be filled by an element imported from the outside; inconsistency, in other words, cannot be equated with *scarcity* of some sort." A discursive tradition remains inconsistent with itself, it turns against itself and in doing so not only undermines itself but also opens up new potentialities for itself. The difficulty that must be resisted, then, is that of seeking to cover over this inconsistency, either by positing a solution from outside or by insisting that the impossibility of such a solution amounts to an intrinsic "scarcity." It is my interest to advance this inconsistency as a differential potentiality, and in this way to think, on the level of signification, and in terms of particular discursive traditions, what Deleuze would call "difference in itself" (*Difference and Repetition*, 181).

begins not with the calling of all discursive traditions to a pre-established norm, but rather with a *problematic* awareness of the irreducibility of a given discursive tradition to such a norm. Only when this sort of intractability to translation is affirmed can genuinely differential relations become constituted. Diaspora names the differentiality of Christianity, and it names the differentiality of Judaism, but it must do so without conflating them—it must, that is, name the differentiality of these respective differentialities (which I have conceived as interparticularity), and it is this second-order differentiality that Yoder's diaspora leaves unthought.

It is in virtue of this failure to consider what I am calling second-order differentiality that Yoder does not consider the possibility of a positive reading of the separation between Judaism and Christianity.[13] He does not, in fact, address the question of whether a good came out of this separation, namely the good of the Jewish discursive tradition. Precisely because this question remains unaddressed, it is possible to maintain suspicion that Yoder laments the difference that has come to exist between Jews and Christians, the difference by which Jews have been able to affirmatively understand their particularity. Boyarin puts this point in his own manner:

> Is there a possibility of an ethics of the preservation of that which is in some genealogical sense, mine, just simply because it is the unique cultural product of the people with whom I choose/have been chosen to be historically connected (a project with which I am not sure that Yoder is in sympathy)? . . . For Yoder the "division" is tragic; I am sure that the division has led to tragedy and that as surely I would want to change, but I still ask whether it is necessary to undo the division to end the tragedy, or possible, perhaps, to comprehend and live it differently.[14]

The only way to affirm diaspora, then, is to refuse its identification with a specific discursive tradition, or with a transcendent norm, while simultaneously insisting on the possibility—or more exactly, the ethical imperative of affirming the possibility—of particular discursive traditions that remain irreducible to one another.[15] It is not that such traditions

13. The argument I am advancing in these paragraphs can be similarly applied to Yoder's discussion, in *Nonviolence* (esp. 22–26), of the parallels between Gandhi's nonviolence and Christian versions of nonviolence.

14. Boyarin, "Judaism as a Free Church," 8.

15. This lack of second-order differentiality also affects Yoder's claim that Christianity

would not be able to speak to one another, it is rather that they can speak to one another and can invent novel relations only insofar as the possibility of their irreducibility to one another is affirmed. The aim of conceiving second-order differentiality is to accede to this possibility, to "live [the difference] differently."

Beginning Without Origin or End

The logic of diaspora allows us to refuse the choice between the transcendent tendency of an identitarian discursive tradition and the purely disruptive tendency of a traditionless difference. This is because it conceives the possibility of traditions that would be able to take seriously their groundlessness—that is, to see their integrity and their groundlessness in a non-competitive manner.[16] The failure of a discursive tradition arises with its incapacity to be affected by the fact that it is a differential composition through and through, that it is originarily problematic—or that it emerges by discerning and constructively responding to a differential problematic. This does not mean that a discursive tradition necessarily falls short of the problematic it discerns. On the contrary, a tradition's

---

is not religious, or cultic, but rather "secular" (See Yoder, *Politics of Jesus*, 39, and *Original Revolution*, 15). While there is a real value in affirming a secular excess beyond the cultic—a value for which I have argued in "Epistemological Violence, Christianity, and the Secular"—there is also a danger, which is that the valorization of secularity may come to write out of existence the particular discursive traditions that appear as cultic. (The danger, in other words, is analogous to the one Boyarin discerns in Yoder's account of diaspora, i.e., that it may write out of existence the particular discursive tradition of Judaism.) The value of Yoder's "secular" Christianity lies in its ability to refuse the otherworldly and thus depoliticizing tendencies of "cultic" Christianity, but this does not mean that such a distinction can then be indifferently applied to other, non-Christian discursive traditions. Indeed, it is precisely this sort of indifferent application that was operative in secularism's invention of the discourse of religion (with religion being understood to include cultic traditions). I would suggest, as an aside, that Yoder's opposition between cultic and secular be replaced by, or at least read through, the opposition he envisions when he notes that it is possible to make a distinction between "'religion' as that which sanctifies and celebrates life as it is, things as they are," and "the category of 'history' [which] represents the morally meaningful particular processes, which may not go in a straight line but at least go somewhere" (*Jewish-Christian Schism Revisited*, 108). If there is anything to be opposed in the cultic, then it will lie most immediately not in its non-secularity, but rather in its refusal of the intrinsic inconsistency, or the contingent potentiality, that is affirmed in those religions that Yoder imagines as historical.

16. I am deeply indebted to conversations with Brian Goldstone regarding this relationship between groundlessness and discursive tradition.

emergence may very well be due to its ability to construct something adequate to the problematic. Yet if a discursive tradition is to remain vital, then it must become capable of beginning again, which is to say it must become immanent to the problematic character of its constitution. An example might be found in the instance of Christianity: on one hand, it calls for the composition of relations that exceed those mandated by imperial power—Pauline thought, I noted, problematizes the universality of "law"—such that the Christian discursive tradition activates new potentialities; on the other, it establishes religion as something it has already solved, the coeval effects of which are to sediment Christian identity and to occlude the potentialities of alternative discursive traditions. The difficulty here is not the existence of discursive tradition as such; it is the imagination of an *identitarian* discursive tradition.

What I am suggesting is that one may discern, in the logic of apocalyptic, a key resource for rendering the discursive tradition of Christianity problematic. Importantly, the logic implicated in apocalyptic is not something that would transcend Christian discourse; it is rather something that one articulates precisely because one is involved in such a discursive tradition.[17] There is no mutual exclusivity between discursive tradition and apocalyptic, here understood as that which would unground the identity of discursive tradition. Apocalyptic is part and parcel of Christian declaration, right from the beginning. From this vantage, Yoder's affirmation of a contingent potentiality of historical existence, one in excess of what is expressed by history-telling, is a creative repetition of Christian declaration: it takes place within Christian discursive tradition, but in such a way that this discursive tradition becomes differential. Furthermore, Yoder's affirmation is apocalyptic, for time bears a potentiality in virtue of which all historical continuity is rendered unnecessary and thus cannot be subjected to the limits of history-telling. The passage from one event to another did not have to be what it was; any continuity espied in such a passage is ungrounded by its contingency, by the potentiality of other passages. To imagine reality in a deeper sense, as Yoder demands, is to imagine the discontinuity of an apocalyptic reality.

This apocalyptic reality, while undoubtedly shaped by a Christian discursive tradition, departs from the apocalyptic reality imagined in Pauline thought. Boyarin observes that the apocalyptic character of Paul's thought

17. Though obviously one may also find and articulate apocalyptic (or something else that would unground identity) within the context of other discursive traditions.

is inseparable from its allegorical character. For Paul, Christ marks a discontinuity in history by revealing something that was not apparent, and it is for this reason that such discontinuity must be apocalyptically understood. However, that which is revealed is something already established: "the true meaning always existed and only waited for the Christ event in order to be revealed."[18] How can it be that something is not present, and yet already established? This is only possible through an allegorical approach, here understood in its ontological valence, which begins by presupposing a substantive separation between a temporal and an eternal plane. The truth revealed in the "Christ event" was already established in the eternal, transcendent plane, but it still needed to be apocalyptically made present in the temporal plane. Apocalyptic thus becomes not an immanent temporal discontinuity, but rather an allegorical participation in the transcendent. Reality in a deeper sense no longer names the forces of an immanent potentiality of time; it instead names that which would transcend time. Once this Pauline move is made, all that is left for historical existence is to participate in history-telling writ large, the allegorical interpretation of time from the vantage of what is beyond time. Paradoxically, the apocalyptic dimension of Pauline thought, though discontinuous with historical existence prior to Christ, ultimately underwrites the invulnerable continuity established by allegorical participation. If apocalyptic and allegory are "homologous," Boyarin adds, it is insofar as both of them "figure an 'end to history.'"[19]

The fact that Pauline apocalyptic nullifies the discontinuous potentiality of time does not, of course, signal a fault inherent to apocalyptic as such. What is necessary is to subtract apocalyptic from the transcendent continuity involved in Pauline allegory, and to do so is to restore apocalyptic to immanence, to time. Yet if apocalyptic liberates the *futurity* of time from history-telling, what about the *primordiality* of time? History-telling must be problematized not only in its futural, but also in its primordial dimension; if there is no end, then neither may there be

18. Boyarin, *Radical Jew*, 35.

19. Ibid. According to Harink's account of Pauline thought—and here he is explicitly following Martyn—it is the case "that the arrival of Jesus Christ into human society and creation is not simply an 'unveiling' of something hidden but always present; rather it is God's *invasion* into a world order enslaved by powers opposed to God's purpose" (*Paul Among the Postliberals*, 122 n. 39). On the account of Pauline thought offered by Boyarin, however, there is no need to accept this binary in which one chooses to interpret apocalyptic either as an "unveiling" or as an "invasion." The former applies insofar as what is revealed was already there at a transcendent or spiritual level, whereas the latter applies insofar as the worldly or material level must be invaded by what is revealed.

an origin. It is precisely such problematizing of origins that we can find in Catherine Keller's work, *The Face of the Deep*, which argues that the Christian doctrine of *creatio ex nihilo* presupposes yet disavows a pre-existing materiality.[20] This is to say that God the Creator is not original, that the activity of divine creation takes place within a pre-creative milieu called chaos. God creates, but when God created, "*the earth was tohu vabohu, and darkness was upon the face of tehom and the ruach elohim was vibrating upon the face of the mayim*."[21] The original creation belies itself insofar as "the chaos is *always already there*";[22] the origin is thus second, it depends on its milieu, namely a "topos of the deep."[23]

Can we not see, in the doctrine of *creatio ex nihilo*, the logic behind history-telling? To say reality originates with a transcendent Creator—transcendent because, as origin, this Creator ontologically precedes what is created—is to ignore that deeper reality discerned by Yoder in "forces which were at work," and similarly discerned by Keller as "tehom," quite literally "the Deep." The denial of discontinuity effected by the allegory of Pauline thought, which gives history an end and cuts off temporal futurity, is echoed in the doctrine of *creatio ex nihilo*, which gives history an origin and cuts off temporal primordiality. It is thus necessary, once again, to affirm the contingent potentiality of time. This is not, however, to replace the origin of a transcendent Creator with the origin of chaos. It is instead to undo the very notion of an origin to which one could refer, and on the basis of which one could ground an identitarian discursive tradition. Keller, like Yoder, resists the identitarian tendencies of Christianity not by refusing all affiliation with its discursive tradition, but rather by re-reading it and thereby opening up its intractable inconsistency. The discursive tradition of Christianity is inconsistent from the beginning, and this is because the beginning it signifies is discontinuous: in the beginning was the discontinuity of chaos and God, of material divergence and creative consistency. Just as there is no need to choose between pure disruption and identitarian traditions, neither is there a need to choose between chaotic excessiveness and formal consistency. Keller considers an interpretation of creation that evades such mutual exclusivity, an interpretation "in which the chaos is neither nothing nor evil; in which to create is not *to master*

20. Keller, *Face of the Deep*.
21. Gen 1:2. Quoted in Keller, *Face of the Deep*, 9. Emphasis in original.
22. Keller, *Face of the Deep*, 9. Emphasis in original.
23. Ibid., 35.

the formless but to solicit its virtual forms."[24] It is precisely this approach that is implied in diaspora, which sees difference neither as something to be sublated in identity nor as something that remains the brute inverse of identity. Diasporic thought sees the chaos of the deep as that which decomposes identitarian forms and enables the re-composition—here the creative solicitation—of differential forms. Indeed, a diasporic account of Christian declaration, which emphasizes that enemy-love means beginning with the signification that exceeds recognition, discovers an ally in Keller's "proposition for any tehomic ethic: *to love is to bear with the chaos.* Not to like it or to foster it but to recognize there the unformed future."[25] An ethic of bearing-with the chaos is the condition of possibility for a diasporic construction of genuinely differential forms. There can be no novelty, no future, without the ability to become subject to that which chaotically exceeds the already established forms.[26] This is to say that the futurity of time is co-mingled with the primordiality of time, with a pre-historical chaos that is apocalyptic with respect to the created. There is neither origin nor end, only an immanently apocalyptic depth of reality—and precisely because of this we may imagine beginnings.[27]

Apocalyptic, of course, has to do with time rather than with space, but (as I proposed in chapter 2) the discontinuity temporally thematized as apocalyptic is the same discontinuity spatially thematized as diaspora. To affirm an apocalyptically characterized Christian discursive tradition is to open the space of diaspora. In fact, the spatial image of Keller's Deep, as a chaos that, while ungrounding, is nonetheless always already *there*, points to the implication of space within the temporality of a discontinuous pre-origin. What, then, does one do with the space opened up by apocalyptic? It is here that we may speak of fabulation, a mode of assembling that runs counter to history-telling.[28] Fabulation, like history-telling, seeks to com-

24. Ibid., 115. Emphasis in original.

25. Ibid., 29. Emphasis in original.

26. Though it should be noted that the chaos need not be something overwhelmingly diffuse, it may very well be a discursive tradition whose consistency cannot be translated into terms already in one's possession.

27. Keller, drawing on the work of Edward Said, makes a similar distinction between origin and becoming in *Face of the Deep*, 162.

28. The concept of fabulation is developed by Deleuze at various points in *Cinema 2*, where it is translated as "story-telling," and by Deleuze and Guattari in *What is Philosophy?*, 167–72. Also related is Deleuze's concept of "the powers of the false"—see *Cinema 2*, 122–50. For an account of how the Bergsonian lineage of the concept of

pose consistencies out of the contingent; unlike history-telling, it does not recognize what it produces as a necessity. This is to say that fabulation understands itself as stemming from the very contingent potentiality that history-telling, in its production of necessity, forecloses. Fabulation is manifestly false, and this is especially apparent in contradistinction to history-telling, which takes its cues from the truth of the course of historical existence. Yet it is precisely because of its manifest falseness that fabulation maintains an alternative power—freed from the retroactive representationalism of history-telling, it is able to weave consistencies out of that which is denied reality by such "truth." Accordingly, while fabulation does not proceed from a truth that history-telling lacks, it does proceed from a potentiality absent in history-telling—and this is because it proceeds from the namelessness of immanence, here spatialized as the Deep, the chaos that is there before anything belonging to history-telling even gets off the ground. The chaotic depth tends to unground more than it grounds, but this does not mean it must simply be left vacant, as some kind of formless wilderness.[29] One needs instead to imagine consistencies of the groundless—and this is what fabulation does. To diasporically compose differential forms, then, is to fabulate relations. These relations do not correspond to already established meanings, for they are new, but this is not to say they come from nothing. They emerge, on the contrary, from that spatial surplus of the Deep—which, as the chaotic depth-milieu of immanence, allows their "falseness" to attain reality.

To fabulate is to imagine diaspora, and thus to signify space apart from the borders of identity by which space, with the aid of history-telling (of origins, ends, and necessities), has been carved up. It is because such signification of space is "apart from" borders, rather than simply "beyond" them, that fabulation cannot be identified with fantasy. Eric Santner has sought to conceive an "exodus" from "a life captured by the question of its legitimacy."[30] The concern of my argument here overlaps with his insofar

---

fabulation can be re-expressed in the contemporary, see Barber and Smith, "Too Poor for Measure," esp. 10–14.

29. The logic that would be involved in such leaving-to-be is one that resembles the biopolitical abandonment of life. This is to say that the biopolitical opposition between *bios* and *zoē*, by which such abandonment is enabled—here I am following the analysis advanced by Giorgio Agamben's *Homo Sacer*—would be structurally homologous with the opposition between the necessity determined by history-telling (with its origins and ends) and the contingent potentiality of the chaotic depth.

30. Santner, *On the Psychotheology of Everyday Life*, 30.

as it can be said that legitimacy is precisely what is at stake in diaspora—after all, to imagine diasporically is to imagine existence apart from the various modes of legitimacy provided by identitarian forms of Christianity and secularism, and by the history-tellings bound up with such identities. Again, then, we come up against this articulation of potentialities of existence in terms of their being "apart from" pre-established identities, or modes of legitimation. Fabulation is meant to conceive the real capacity to proceed "apart from," but to do so in such a manner that this capacity is not grounded in something beyond. Santner, in attempting to make the same sort of distinction, makes clear that the exodus he conceives is "not one from ordinary life into a space beyond it but in a sense just the opposite: a release from the fantasies that keep us in the thrall of some sort of exceptional beyond."[31]

Accordingly, it is important to insist that fabulation be understood, quite precisely, as that which emerges in the aftermath of problematization, of the becoming-chaotic of pre-established identities. If fantasy names the support of identity, if it is what enables identity to withstand the threats that contingent potentiality' poses to fixation on origins and ends, then fabulation will differ from fantasy only insofar as it begins from the problematic—that is, from the dissolution of such identity and its fantastic support. Diaspora is what separates fantasy and fabulation; it is the affirmation of the relays across and fractures within the boundaries that legitimate—in fact, it is through this tendency to valorize what is denied legitimacy (or to draw on Santner's nuance, what has its legitimacy called into question) that diaspora affirms that something is *there*, irreducible to legitimating identities. I have conceived this "something *there*" through the notion of a chaotic depth precisely because of its refusal to be beyond. Affirmation of the depth is not affirmation of something beyond signification, it is affirmation of something interstitial to signification; its space does not transcend the space of the world, it is instead the deterritorialization of the selfsame space that is subjected to legitimation. This is what it means to be "apart from." Diasporic fabulation is thus the naming of what is apart, of what Santner names as "the remnant" and defines as "the part that is not a part of a whole but rather the opening beyond the 'police order' of parts and wholes."[32] It is a fabulation not of what would be

31. Ibid., 30–31. He further describes his interest as follows: "I am suggesting that the task of truly inhabiting the 'midst of life' involves the risk of an unbinding or loosening of this fantasy as well as the social bond effectuated in it" (33).

32. Ibid., 142.

beyond affliction, of something that would restore a prior state of health (origin) or ultimately resolve our problematic existence (end), but rather of something that is still there, that remains in the aftermath of affliction and thus poses the potentiality of an existence apart from such affliction.[33] Fabulation, in other or words, is nothing more and nothing less than the experimentation with this kind of potentiality.

The Differentiality of Differentialities: Christianity, Religion, and the Secular

What I am proposing—to make matters explicit—is that Christianity, when it foregrounds its apocalyptic character, finds itself constitutively dispersed, such that to be committed to it is to be committed to a diasporic existence. To say that this dispersal is *constitutive* is to say that the tradition exists not as a ground of identity that then requires dispersal, but rather as dispersal itself. The Christian discursive tradition is differential from the very beginning, which means that it exists only by beginning again. It is not, in other words, a product of history-telling; it is instead a product of fabulation—and if it exists only as fabulation, which always stems from ungrounding, then its existence depends on its ability to become ungrounded, to "bear with the chaos." Yet what I have in mind here is not some peculiarly Christian paradox whereby identity and un-grounding circle about one another incessantly. On the contrary, what I am asserting about Christianity would hold for any discursive tradition. The depth of space poses a chaotic potentiality that ungrounds any iden-titarian form; it presents an immanent reality that is common to each and every tradition that it exceeds. Furthermore, the chaos is not an ahistorical paradox of identity. Chaos refers to the differential character of material singularities; it is the spatial surplus that makes possible, yet ungrounds, the discourse that constitutes a tradition. The proper response to this ungrounding, then, is not to vertically contemplate a paradoxical clench of tradition and ungrounding, it is rather to horizontally decompose and recompose spatial relations.

33. It would be possible to begin thinking the double relay of Spinoza's "God, or Nature," from the vantage of this "something that is still there"—which is to say that what I am trying to imagine, by way of a diasporic "apart from," is something neither simply philosophical nor simply theological.

To conceive this chaos as the sheer negation of form, or more broadly of tradition, is to fall into transcendence; to ignore it in the name of a pre-established form or tradition is to turn it into nothing. History-telling fears the former and affirms the latter, but fabulation evades both errors by composing chaos, by approaching forms and traditions diasporically. That which is rendered false by identitarian forms and discursive traditions gains the power to become true through the fabulative composition of a pre-original, and thus pre-grounded, spatial depth of reality.

But why, if this proposal applies to each and every discursive tradition, have I focused on Christianity? It is because of the central role that Christianity has played in engendering the mode of domination that still remains with us, even as Christianity is no longer regnant. This mode of domination, of course, is not strictly equivalent to Christianity, for it exists through and as the deployment of a triadic relation of difference in which Christianity is but one term. Nonetheless, this triad of terms gets off the ground with the invention of Christianity. Accordingly, if Christianity does not name a substantive identity, then the differential deployed in the mode of domination cannot hold up. My interest is therefore not to redeem us from domination in the name of pure Christianity, but rather to unground this mode of domination by ungrounding one of its constitutive elements, namely an identitarian Christian discursive tradition. I am, in other words, re-dramatizing the sickness in hope of mimetic cure. It is still possible to speak of a Christian discursive tradition, but it will be one that is inconsistent, or differential, from the beginning. This diasporic Christianity is fabulative from beginning to end, and as such it cannot become the established support of that which will be identified with a concomitantly and equally established religion. Neither can it provide the model for that which will be consequently established, under the guise of secularism, as that which overcomes religion. To put it otherwise: if Christianity is fabulation all the way down, then it loses the ability to generate the history-telling enacted by the mode of domination; if Christianity is a diasporic composition dependent on an ungrounding, differentially emerging depth of reality, then it cannot ground the identity required by the mode of domination.

We may, in this respect, consider the possibility of distinguishing the Christian discursive tradition from the discursive *field* of the mode of domination. This discursive field, as I have argued, must be understood as a relation of differences: first, between the "true" Christian religion and all other (non-Christian) religions, and second, between the secular and the religious. What I am proposing is a delinking of the Christian discursive tradition from the mode of domination's discursive field, a delinking made possible by a diasporic, fabulative account of this tradition. Christianity can enter the differential field only under the condition that it names an identity—an identity, furthermore, that underwrites the identity of religion, and concomitantly the difference between proper religion and improper religions. The difference inherent to the mode of domination's discursive field thus requires the establishment of an identitarian Christianity, whereas a diasporic Christianity affirms a difference that is prior to the difference that emerges between one (religious) identity and other (religious) identities. What, then, of religion and of the secular? If it is possible to imagine a Christianity that, because it is intrinsically differential, evades the identity that is then differentially deployed in the mode of domination's discursive field, is it also possible to imagine accounts of religion and the secular that would likewise (though in their own manner) articulate a difference irreducible to their capture by this discursive field? What is at stake, in other words, is the conception of differences not just within Christianity, but also within religion and within the secular, that would render each term internally inconsistent and thus unable to support the differences between Christian identity, religious identity, and secular identity. When these differences-within are affirmed, diaspora emerges, once again, as the differentiality of differentialities—though in this case the differentialities refer not to Christianity and Judaism, but to Christianity, religion, and the secular—such that the three concepts at issue cannot be captured by the differentiality of identities deployed in the mode of domination's discursive field. I have already pointed to the possibility of differentiality within the concept of Christianity, and so in what remains I will briefly point to the possibility of differentialities with the concepts of religion and the secular.

If a differential concept of religion is to be imagined, then it will be necessary, above all, to refuse heresiology, which was the enabling condition for the establishment of identitarian Christianity as normative religion. Christianity recognized its identity through the naming of a heretical outside, and it recognized itself as proper religion through the naming of other, improper religions. The essences of Christianity and religion are in this sense intertwined, even mutually constitutive—but note that this identification of Christianity and religion can only take place against a backdrop of difference *between* Christian religions and other religions. There must be, in the first place, objects capable of being identified as religions, and this identification itself takes place by dint of heresiology. It is for this reason, then, that Christianity did not just name its own heresies but sought, in addition, heresies in relation to the object of Judaism.[34] If there are no heresies of Judaism, then Judaism is not easily identified as a religion; if Judaism is not a religion, then the identity of Christianity as proper religion is called into question. Heresiology produces Christianity, but it does so only insofar as it is also able to produce identifiable things called religion.

How does one then proceed, if one does not want to become inscribed within the borders of religious identities? One path would involve opposing religion as such. The apparent advantage of this option derives from awareness of the link between the concept of religion and the dominance of identitarian Christianity. If one wishes to evade such dominance, does it not become compelling to refuse that thing called religion through which domination is established? Compelling though this option may be, it encounters the notable difficulty that it has already been tried under the guise of secularism—it is, after all, the precise move of secularism to promise redemption from Christian domination under the guise of redemption from religion in general. This brings about the end of *Christian* domination, but it does not bring about the end of domination as such. If anything, the relations of domination remain constant: Christianity is superseded by the secular, but association with an object of (non-Christian) religion still tends to put one in a position of subjection. It is in virtue of this fact that the option of straightforwardly refusing religion loses its allure. One could, in fact, see a strange recapitulation of heresiology in the secular supersession of Christianity. It is as if secularism, in order to break free of a heresiological Christianity, had to enact its own heresiology, such that those who are religious become the heretics

34. Boyarin, making reference to the alleged list of Jewish heresies of which Justin Martyr claims to know, contends "that through this elaboration of a *Jewish* heresiology . . . Justin was doing work of his own. That work could have been an early adumbration of the discursive strategy that was to become fully elaborated by the end of the fourth century: that of distinguishing from the Christian side an orthodox Judaism as the true 'other' of Christianity, such that two binary pairs are put into place, Judaism/Christianity and heresy/orthodoxy, with Judaism, both supporting through semiotic opposition the notion of an autonomous Christianity, and being itself an orthodoxy, also serving to mark the semantic distinction between orthodoxy and heresy" (*Border Lines*, 43).

of secularism; secularism recognizes itself, it constitutes its identity, by naming its heretical outside as religion.

There is, of course, a certain peculiarity in associating heresiology with something that explicitly separates itself from religion. Yet, without denying this peculiarity, it is important to propose such an association. This is because the operation enacted by heresiology, despite emerging in a religious context, does not *require* such a context. To be a heretic is to have an "other" belief, a commitment that renders one outside the norm and thus helps constitute the identifiability of this norm. As long as Christendom is dominant, to be a heretic, to have an "other" belief, is to be religious in the wrong manner; when secularism becomes dominant, to have an "other" belief is simply to be religious. Does this mean that religion becomes heresy? Not if we consider heresy in the strict sense of being religious in the wrong way. In a broader sense, however, the term is helpful, because it foregrounds the manner in which the flight from Christian religion is not equivalent to the flight from the valorization of domination over those who maintain false beliefs. We surrender to a blind spot when we imagine that the operation referred to under the term "heresiology" disappears once Christian religion ceases to be ascendant. The Christian religion that invents heresiology is superseded, but it may very well be the case that this supersession is established in the same manner that what is superseded was established. What is pressing, then, is not the refusal of religion; it is the refusal of heresiology—the object of antagonism must be given precision. To refuse heresiology is to refuse the tendency towards the identitarian when it occurs in religion, but also when it occurs outside religion, such as it does in secularism. It is important, in other words, to evade a flat dismissal of anything interpellated as religion, and this is because religion is not univocal—it may name something that aims to dominate others, but it may just as well name those others that are subject to such an aim. If we wish to conceive religion outside of these relations of domination, then we will have to avoid a simple valorization of or opposition to religion. We must conceive religion in an unrestricted sense—that is, apart from the restrictions engendered by a normative Christianity, which provides the essence of religion, and by a normative secular, which likewise essentializes religion (inversely) as that which falls outside of its own domain.

Religion, once it is delinked from heresiology, may be affirmed. I previously noted Schwartz's claim that religion, in the epoch of Christianization, became inseparable from a process of disembedding. What I am proposing here is an affirmation of religion's capacity to disembed, or to deterritorialize. This has special relevance with regard to the secular, which tends to present itself as clearing away extraneous, inessential modes of belief or ritual practice in the name of adequation to a clear picture of reality.[35] For immanence, however, reality is excessive—there is a surplus of reality, a chaotic depth that cannot ever be adequately described by way of referential adequation. What is lost in the secular proscription on religious discourse is the affirmation of such surplus. This is not to propose that religion discovers the truth that secularism fails to describe—not at all, for as I have just claimed this sort of truth is impossible to achieve. Religion does, however, maintain a relation to the surplus that secularism denies in the name of its search for a clear picture of reality.[36] What therefore ends up falling under the concept of religion—at least insofar as it is dialectically opposed to the secular—is immanent excess.

Yet if the concept of religion is to function in favor of a disembedding of the secular's clear picture of reality, then it must be able to do so without being positioned in relation *to* the secular. It is not enough, in other words, just to say that religion poses a difference against the secular; it must also become possible to imagine religion as being differential in itself (much as Christianity, in order to evade the differential relations of the mode of domination, must be understood as intrinsically inconsistent). An indication of this possibility can be glimpsed in Masuzawa's treatment of Max Müller's somewhat idiosyncratic (or "unscientific") insistence, in his *Introduction to the Science of Religion*, on including the "Turanian," alongside the "Semitic" and the "Aryan," within his classification of language groups. What is peculiar about this "Turanian" group, according to Masuzawa's account, is that it is defined, first and foremost, by what it is not. In other words, while the Aryan and Semitic groups possess, in

35. Asad is drawn to Margaret Canovan's image of liberalism as the establishment of a garden amidst an otherwise feral milieu. "The image Canovan employs to present and defend liberalism is striking: 'making a garden in a jungle that is continually encroaching' and a 'world [that] is a dark place, which needs redemption by the light of a myth'" (*Formations of the Secular*, 59). While he reads this mythical imagination of the garden as a justification of liberalism's violence (against the ever-straying fecundity of the jungle), I believe it may be understood to indicate, more broadly, the secular valorization of a (seemingly Cartesian) clear and distinct picture of reality. Whatever is then too unkempt or indistinct, whatever lacks the aspiration towards translucence, falls under religion.

36. This, it should be noted, is not due to some peculiar characteristic of an essence of religion—if religion maintains this relation to surplus, it is because the secular names excess as religion.

their respective manners, characteristics that refer to specific peoples and languages, the Turanian group is without its own similarly determinate reference. Masuzawa cites, to this effect, some comments made by Müller: "the characteristic marks of union [of the Turanian group], ascertained for its immense variety of language, are as yet very vague and general, if compared with the definite ties of relationship which severally unite the Semitic and the Arian."[37] Clearly, then, the Turanian lacks the sort of empirical referentiality possessed by the other groups with which it is compared. Does this compromise the validity of the Turanian? It must, as long as the criteria of empirical science are upheld—but it may be that what Müller was seeking under the category of the Turanian was something pre-empirical, something like the condition of possibility for linguistic consistency. Masuzawa claims that, for Müller, the "very diffuseness" of the Turanian becomes its "distinct characteristic," and this is evident, she observes, in Müller's assertion that "Turanian dialects . . . are *Nomadic languages* as contrasted with the Arian and Semitic dialects, which may be called *State* or *political languages.*"[38]

What is the meaning—or the ethical import—of Müller's peculiar insistence on the Turanian? Masuzawa argues that his aim is to resist the racialization of language groups. Without denying this, and without claiming to discern Müller's actual intentions, I would suggest that there is yet another insight to be grasped. The account of linguistic origins that Müller is providing, it should be noted, is also an account of religious origins; the science of religious groups, for him, is inseparable from the science of language groups. Indeed, let us not forget that what is at issue in this science is the founding of secular discourse on religion, of the discourse that allows secularism to know and thus supersede its religious others. This link between language and religion, the knowledge of which is at the heart of the attempt to demarcate the secular from the religious, makes all the more intriguing Müller's claim that the reason Turanian dialects remain diffuse is their lack of a support in a state, which is also to say their lack of a religious support. If Aryan and Semitic languages have a clear empirical referent, this is owing to the fact that they have been able to "hand down a language," an operation that "is possible only among people whose history runs on in one main stream; and where religion, law, and poetry supply well-defined borders which hem in on every side the current of

37. Masuzawa, *Invention of World Religions,* 230.
38. Ibid.

language."[39] Turanian languages, on the other hand, lack such political and religious support. They lack borders that would render them recognizable. As an historical account, this binary between the Aryan-Semitic and the Turanian is difficult to accept, yet it seems possible to interpret it transcendentally (as a difference affecting the concept prior to its empirical confirmation): the Turanian lacks linguistic-religious identity, but this does not mean it is nothing; its inability to achieve identity indicates a reality that exceeds the very concept of religiously supported peoples, a reality that precedes and thus conditions the emergence of such peoples.

What, then, is this excess? It is not enough to say that it is the excess of the religious to the secular, for this sort of excess is already measured by the invention of the secular concept of religion—an invention to which Müller's efforts were, in fact, contributing. It is something else, namely the excess of religion to itself; religion does not just deterritorialize a dialectically opposed secular identity, it also deterritorializes the very identity of religion. The Turanian ungrounds the attempt to conceive the origins of religion, and so its relation to religious identity can be understood as being analogous to the relation of the Deep to Christian identity—in each case, inconsistency emerges not as the effect of, but rather as the condition for, discernible consistencies. Furthermore, and importantly for the purposes of escaping the differential relations established by the mode of domination, the non-religious character of the Turanian does not coincide with the non-religious character of the secular: the secular separates itself from religion through supersession, whereas the Turanian separates itself from religion by naming a pre-religious milieu whose value resides neither in being religious nor in being secular. One might say, drawing on Müller's claim that its dialects, insofar as they lack a religious support, are "Nomadic," that the Turanian has an excessive relation to linguistic sense.[40] While religion and the secular have their own peculiar senses, the

---

39. Ibid., 232.

40. It is worth noting the peculiar resonance between Müller's account of the nomadic and Deleuze and Guattari's own affirmation of the nomadic: "If the nomad can be called the Deterritorialized par excellence, it is precisely because there is no reterritorialization *afterward* as with the migrant, or upon *something else* as with the sedentary (the sedentary's relation with the earth is mediatized by something else, a property regime, a State apparatus). With the nomad, on the contrary, it is deterritorialization that constitutes the relation to the earth, to such a degree that the nomad reterritorializes on deterritorialization itself. . . . They are vectors of deterritorialization. They add desert to desert, steppe to steppe, by a series of local operations whose orientation and direction

lack of an analogous sense with regard to the Turanian indicates an excessive use of language, such that the Turanian proceeds from a nonsense that, because it is prior to sense, must be understood as the "*donation of sense*."[41] The Turanian conceives, against identitarian modes of conceptuality, the contingent potentiality of an existence that refuses to engage in a history-telling that "runs on in one main stream."

It should be clear, in the wake of this account of the inconsistency of religion, that I am not advocating an inversion of the secular, such that something called religion becomes valuable and secularity loses all value. I am arguing, more precisely, that the conceptual opposition between the secular and the religious must be displaced (a displacement indicated, for instance, by Müller's account of the Turanian), and that this is because it diverts thought from what matters most: the potentialities of existence. It is certainly the case that religion can underwrite identitarian forms—but I am not calling for the affirmation of religion as such anymore than I am calling for the refusal of religion as such. Secularism tends to present us with a false binary whereby we must choose either the restriction of religion or the potentiality for becoming opened up by the liberation from religion. This opposition is mistaken, for the real antagonism lies not between secularism and religion but between heresiological and non-heresiological modes of existence. Potentiality must be affirmed, but such potentiality may in fact be exercised by what is interpellated as religion, or by what, following Müller, is nomadically (and perhaps diasporically) prior to religion. Concomitantly, the annihilation of potentiality may in fact be enacted by the secular interpellation and restriction of its religious others.

The object of antagonism, in this case, is neither the secular nor religion; it is more exactly the discursive field that differentiates them as mutually exclusive terms. What matters is learning to see the nonidentity between these terms, and while the perception of such nonidentity may require a turning of religion against the secular, and of the secular against religion, this is not because we are tending towards a third term that would synthesize them. We are tending, on the contrary, towards a differential, immanent relay between two initially separated terms. Diaspora stands

---

endlessly vary" (*A Thousand Plateaus*, 421). For both Deleuze and Guattari's nomads and Müller's Turanian, what is central is deterritorialization.

41. Deleuze, in *Logic of Sense*, 69, remarks: "No less than the determination of signification, nonsense enacts a *donation of sense*." Emphasis in original.

against the separation of the secular and the religious not only at the level of practical exercise—whereby it composes relations drawing upon both recognizably secular and religious elements—but also at the level of the conceptual. This is to say that the concept of diaspora affirms something irreducibly secular as well as something irreducibly religious, but in such a manner that any process of decomposition and recomposition must involve both. Diaspora is able to affirm religion *in principle* insofar as it adopts a thoroughly non-reductive approach to signification. Religion, in this sense, is understood to be emerging from the excess of immanence as an inconsistency irreducible to the secular, and thus as an enactment of the capacity to fabulate (a capacity recognized in Müller's own fabulation of the Turanian). Such a production of signification can, of course, go badly—it can sediment itself through a heresiological operation, it can make its discourse into a mode of transcendence. Yet this occurrence only highlights the need to delink religion from heresiology and thereby to unhinge the signification of a religion's discursive tradition from the tendency towards transcendence, such that a discursive tradition would affirm its own link to "the Turanian." The demand to affirm religion—a religion, once again, that is capable of being deterritorialized by its "Turanian" valence and thus of affirming its intrinsic inconsistency—stems from the necessity of signifying the excessive namelessness of immanence.

As I argued at the outset, however, the necessity of excessively signifying must be relayed, or immanently doubled, by the necessity of conceiving the proper namelessness of immanence, or the impropriety of excessive signification. It is this latter necessity, then, that issues the demand to delink signification (and its expression in discursive traditions) from the tendency towards transcendence—it is also, more positively, what issues the demand to affirm secularity. This concept of secularity should be understood as precisely as possible: it does not indicate the opposition to religion, or even the reformation of religion; it indicates the fundamentally immanent orientation of all signification, such that the improper—and thus truly excessive—character of signification is affirmed. If an intrinsically differential concept of religion indicates the immeasurability of signification, then an intrinsically differential concept of secularity indicates the immeasurability of namelessness. Yet in order to understand how secularity is intrinsically differential we must first distinguish secularity from the imagination of a secular plane. The difficulty with the latter resides in its conversion of namelessness into transcendence. When this takes place, secularity defines itself negatively as that which has stripped itself from (religious) signification. In doing so, however, it makes the namelessness it rightly affirms into its own mode of signification; it forms a discursive tradition that sediments namelessness into a positive figure and in the process cuts itself off from the very contingent potentiality in virtue of which it reveals the impropriety of signification. Secularity must not become auto-referential, which is to say that it must not understand itself as something achieved (much less as something achieved by a particular culture).[42] There is no secular plane, only an immanent plane that is expressed and constructed by signification. The power of secularity, then, lies not in converting this immanent plane into a self-consciously secular plane. Immanence is already nameless; it does not need this namelessness to be posited—such positing, in fact, turns the truth of namelessness into an idol, it does not let the power of namelessness be what it will be.

Secularity, as I am conceiving it, would involve not the installation of a secular plane, but rather the exercise of a power of namelessness already in movement in the one and only plane of immanence. This determination of secularity has implications for its relation to signification, or to the many particular networks of signification that constitute just as many discursive traditions. Specifically, it implies that secularity is not something to be imposed upon networks of signification, such that secularity would provide proper limits of their exercise or invariants that articulate a least common denominator among their variations. The value of secularity does reside in its affirmation of commonality; it is just that this commonality cannot be posited as something that would be named as the secular. What is common to all networks of signification, or particularities, is the contingent potentiality of namelessness, but this namelessness must emerge interstitially—in the interstices between particularities, as well as in the interstices of each particular discursive tradition.[43] The demand

42. In this sense I am in agreement with Toscano's criticism (*Fanaticism*, 100) of "current invocations of the Enlightenment" that are "complicit with the culturalization of rationality." This, he notes, has the effect of stripping the "daring, discipline and risk" involved in Enlightenment by making it "as if we already know what reason and emancipation entailed" and erecting "a picture of the Enlightenment as a precious possession, to be secured and defended."

43. It is because such a view of the common—or really of the operation of "commoning"—is committed to irreducible differentiality and to the refusal of any manner of mediation from above that it is able to resonate with the theory of "the multitude" that Michael Hardt and Antonio Negri first advanced in *Empire*. For both diaspora and

that secularity sets forth, then, is twofold: it is, first, to become exposed to these interstitial differentialities, such that their disavowal in the name of pre-established identities is precluded; it is, second, to understand all of these particularities as immanent to one another, such that no ultimate hierarchies may be established between them. Secularity thus emerges as the demand for an interparticular existence. It is in virtue of this distinctive characteristic, then, that it is intrinsically inconsistent, for it has no identity outside of the differential relations between particularities that are themselves intraparticularly differential.

---

multitude, what is sought is a mode of collectivity that is "in common" without being thinkable in terms of a unified body, such as "the people." This is to say that in each case divergence is seen as central to, rather than as the ruin of, commonality.

Epilogue

THE FACT THAT MY argument has constantly spoken of differentialities and inconsistencies, of the in-between of concepts by which various identities are located, may very well have generated, for the reader, a pointed question: From what position is this written? Where is this argument to be located? I would like, at least in part, to avoid this question, or at least to avoid its presuppositions. Does not the very nature of diaspora resist the idea that meaning must be positioned within an initially recognizable identity? The force of this last question, I think, should not be brushed off as (merely) rhetorical. It should be allowed to put pressure on the assumption that location is found in an originary identity. At the same time, I should confess that I think this pressure can only go so far, that at a certain point it can become a bit precious. So while I insist it is not necessary to position my argument in a pre-existing identity, I agree that it remains necessary to ask about the kind of position one enters if one assents to my argument. What sort of position is being affirmed, or pointed towards, by this book?

Part of the answer to this question is supplied by the argument itself—the position to which it leads is the position that is generated as an effect of the argument. Yet another part of the answer concerns the issue of persona—that is, what sort of persona might one adopt if one thinks according to diaspora? There will, of course, have to be many personae. That said, and without contravening this need for a multitude of personae, I would like to call to mind Spinoza, who was first invoked as a kind of persona in the conclusion of chapter 1. We are, by now, used to imagining the persona of Spinoza in various manners—a liberal Spinoza, a radical Enlightenment Spinoza, a communist Spinoza, a philosophical Spinoza,

146

a quasi-religious Spinoza, an atheist Spinoza . . . and I would submit that there is a diasporic Spinoza. He was, after all, a figure who was both within and without Judaism, Christianity, and the secular, a figure who was a philosopher yet also an inheritor and creative recapitulator of theological traditions. If we are able to recognize him, today, as a singular figure, this is because of the peculiar way that he was able to inhabit all of these positions without ultimately being defined by them. He did not transcend these identities so much as he composed them, pushing them to and beyond their limits without establishing a new position that would be easily recognizable (hence our ability to variously position him). The persona of Spinoza is different because it is differential. Now what ultimately matters here is not whether the diasporic Spinoza is the "true" Spinoza so much as whether we are able, from the vantage of our contemporary conjuncture and in view of the argument that I make, to imagine him as diasporic. It is a matter of differentially repeating, here and now, the persona that Spinoza adopted in his own historical moment. The position I am advancing is, at the very least, one in which such a diasporic persona may be encountered, imagined, and variously inhabited.

To put my point somewhat differently: Our moment is one in which, due to the present modality of global capitalism, value is becoming increasingly abstract. This does not, however, mean that discourses of supposedly "cultural" values, and of the differences between these various sets of values, have subsided. It could be said, on the contrary, that the imagination of a certain, generally reactionary, kind of cultural value fits rather smoothly with a globalizing abstraction of value. They form a relay. What I have been after in this book is the possibility of another manner of relay—one, it might be said, that would not side with either the particularity of a "cultural" value or the universalizing value of the abstract, but that would instead affirm both the inevitable force of signification and the power of a disembedding namelessness. The possibility of such a relay—as it is articulated in interparticularity, or in the mutual reciprocity of namelessness and the excessive, fictive signification of this namelessness, or in the differentiality of differentialities—seems especially pressing.

Santner, in commenting on Franz Rosenzweig's theory of the work of art, observes that "a work's reception cannot be reduced to the unfolding of the inner logic of the work, the bringing to light of what is already in the work as a potential waiting to be actualized."[1] He claims, furthermore, that

1. Santner, *On the Psychotheology of Everyday Life*, 132.

if this means the work is "inexhaustible," then it is not due to finitude, it is not "because . . . the limits of every human consciousness" create a need for "multiple readings to 'bring it out.'"[2] The point is rather that the work is internally inconsistent, or differential, such that its value is to be found, as it were, "outside" of it, constituted after the fact through reception (a manner of reverse causality). Even an omniscient receiver of the work would, through the act of reception, create a value of the work that the work did not already possess. What I am suggesting, then, is that immanence, in its namelessness and excessive signification, in its simultaneous production and disembedding of names (Christianity, religion, and the secular, among others), is like such a work of art. There is no proper way of naming the value, for every value "brought out" of immanence will be improperly excessive, and yet it is precisely this relay, this thoroughly differential milieu, that enables the creation of value—or values. What is common is neither the abstract, universalizing value nor the embedded, culturally signified value; it is instead the relay between them, the capacity to be affected by and to affect this relay. This, I should add, is what I imagine the persona called "diasporic Spinoza" understands. Such a persona is distinguished by its ability to position itself in diaspora, in a position that knows how to make beginnings.

2. Ibid., 133.

Bibliography

Agamben, Giorgio. *Homo Sacer: Sovereign Power and Bare Life*. Translated by Daniel Heller-Roazen. Stanford, CA: Stanford University Press, 1998.

Alliez, Éric. *The Signature of the World, or, What is Deleuze and Guattari's Philosophy?* Translated by Eliot Ross Albert and Alberto Toscano. London: Continuum, 2004.

Anidjar, Gil. *The Jew, the Arab: A History of the Enemy*. Stanford, CA: Stanford University Press, 2003.

————. *Semites: Race, Religion, Literature*. Stanford, CA: Stanford University Press, 2008.

Asad, Talal. *Formations of the Secular: Christianity, Islam, Modernity*. Stanford, CA: Stanford University Press, 2003.

————. *The Idea of an Anthropology of Islam*. Washington, DC: Center for Contemporary Arab Studies, Georgetown University, 1986.

Barber, Daniel Colucciello. "Epistemological Violence, Christianity, and the Secular." In *The New Yoder*, edited by Peter Dula and Chris K. Huebner, 271–93. Eugene, OR: Cascade, 2010.

————. "The Particularity of Jesus and the Time of the Kingdom: Philosophy and Theology in Yoder." *Modern Theology* 23 (2007) 63–89.

Barber, Daniel Colucciello, and Anthony Paul Smith. "Too Poor for Measure: Working with Negri on Poverty and Fabulation." *Journal for Cultural and Religious Theory* 10:3 (2010) 1–15.

Barth, Karl. *The Church and the Political Problem of Our Day*. New York: Scribner, 1939.

————. *Church Dogmatics* I/2. Edited by G. W. Bromiley and T. F. Torrance. Edinburgh: T. & T. Clark, 2000.

Bell, Daniel M., Jr. *Just War as Christian Discipleship: Recentering the Tradition in the Church Rather Than the State*. Grand Rapids: Brazos, 2009.

Benedict XVI. "Papal Address at University of Regensburg." No pages. Online: http://www.zenit.org/article-16955?l=english.

Boyarin, Daniel. *Border Lines: The Partition of Judaeo-Christianity*. Philadelphia: University of Pennsylvania Press, 2004.

————. "Judaism as a Free Church." In *The New Yoder*, edited by Peter Dula and Chris K. Huebner, 1–17. Eugene, OR: Cascade, 2010.

————. *A Radical Jew: Paul and the Politics of Identity*. Berkeley: University of California Press, 1994.

Buell, Denise Kimber. *Why This New Race: Ethnic Reasoning in Early Christianity*. New York: Columbia University Press, 2005.

Carter, J. Kameron. *Race: A Theological Account*. Oxford: Oxford University Press, 2008.

Critchley, Simon. "Mystical Anarchism." *Critical Horizons* 10:2 (2009) 272–306.

Crockett, Clayton, Creston Davis, and Slavoj Žižek, editors. *Hegel and the Infinite: Religion, Politics, and Dialectic*. New York: Columbia University Press, 2011.

Deleuze, Gilles. *Cinema 2: The Time Image*. Translated by Hugh Tomlinson and Robert Galeta. London: Continuum, 2005.

———. *Difference and Repetition*. Translated by Paul Patton. London: Continuum, 2004.

———. *Expressionism in Philosophy: Spinoza*. Translated by Martin Joughin. New York: Zone, 1992.

———. *Logic of Sense*. Translated by Mark Lester with Charles Stivale. New York: Columbia University Press, 1990.

Deleuze, Gilles, and Félix Guattari. *A Thousand Plateaus: Capitalism and Schizophrenia*. Translated by Brian Massumi. London: Continuum, 2004.

———. *What is Philosophy?* Translated by Hugh Tomlinson and Graham Burchell. New York: Columbia University Press, 1996.

Gangle, Rocco. "Theology of the Chimera: Spinoza, Immanence, Practice." In *After the Postsecular and the Postmodern: New Essays in Continental Philosophy of Religion*, edited by Anthony Paul Smith and Daniel Whistler, 30–47. Newcastle upon Tyne: Cambridge Scholars, 2010.

Goodchild, Philip. *Capitalism and Religion: The Price of Piety*. London: Routledge, 2002.

Hardt, Michael, and Antonio Negri. *Empire*. Cambridge: Harvard University Press, 2001.

Harink, Douglas. *Paul Among the Postliberals: Pauline Theology beyond Christendom and Modernity*. Grand Rapids: Brazos, 2003.

Heidegger, Martin. *Introduction to Metaphysics*. Translated by Richard Polt and Gregory Fried. New Haven: Yale University Press, 2000.

———. "Phenomenology and Theology." Translated by James G. Hart and John C. Maraldo. In *Pathmarks*, edited by William McNeill, 39–62. Cambridge: Cambridge University Press, 1998.

Hess, Jonathan. *Germans, Jews, and the Claims of Modernity*. New Haven, CT: Yale University Press, 2002.

Kallenberg, Brad J. *Ethics as Grammar: Changing the Postmodern Subject*. Notre Dame, IN: University of Notre Dame Press, 2001.

Kant, Immanuel. *The Conflict of the Faculties*. Translated by Mary J. Gregor. Lincoln: University of Nebraska Press, 1992.

Keller, Catherine. *Face of the Deep: A Theology of Becoming*. London: Routledge, 2003.

Kerr, Nathan. *Christ, History and Apocalyptic: The Politics of Christian Mission*. Theopolitical Visions 4. Eugene, OR: Cascade, 2008.

King, Richard. *Orientalism and Religion: Postcolonial Theory, India, and "The Mystic East."* London: Routledge, 1999.

Kordela, A. Kiarina. *$urplus: Spinoza, Lacan*. Albany: State University of New York Press, 2007.

Mahmood, Saba. *Politics of Piety: The Islamic Revival and the Feminist Subject*. Princeton, NJ: Princeton University Press, 2005.

———. "Secularism, Hermeneutics, and Empire: The Politics of Islamic Reformation." *Public Culture* 18:2 (2006) 323–47.

Martyn, J. Louis. *Galatians: A New Translation with Introduction and Commentary*. New York: Doubleday, 1997.

Masuzawa, Tomoko. *The Invention of World Religions: Or, How European Universalism Was Preserved in the Language of Pluralism*. Chicago: University of Chicago Press, 2005.

Milbank, John. *Theology and Social Theory: Beyond Secular Reason*. Oxford: Blackwell, 1990.

Mullarkey, John. *Post-Continental Philosophy: An Outline*. London: Continuum, 2006.

Ostashevsky, Eugene. "Now the Lord Said to DJ Spinoza." In *The Life and Opinions of DJ Spinoza*, 97. Brooklyn: Ugly Duckling, 2008.

Rubenstein, Mary-Jane. "Capital Shares: The Way Back into the With of Christianity." *Political Theology* 11 (2010) 103–19.

Santner, Eric. *On the Psychotheology of Everyday Life: Reflections on Freud and Rosenzweig*. Chicago: University of Chicago Press, 2001.

Schwartz, Seth. *Imperialism and Jewish Society, 200 B.C.E. to 640 C.E.* Princeton, NJ: Princeton University Press, 2001.

Siggelkow, Ry O. "Just War Is *Not* Christian Discipleship: A Review of Daniel Bell Jr.'s *Just War*." In *The Other Journal*. No pages. Online: http://theotherjournal.com/2010/05/04/just-war-is-not-christian-discipleship-a-review-of-daniel-bell-jr-s-just-war/.

Smith, Steven B. *Spinoza's Book of Life: Freedom and Redemption in the* Ethics. New Haven: Yale University Press, 2003.

Spinoza. *Ethics*. Edited and translated by Edwin Curley. New York: Penguin, 1996.

Surin, Kenneth. *Freedom Not Yet: Liberation and the Next World Order*. Durham, NC: Duke University Press, 2009.

Taubes, Jacob. *Occidental Eschatology*. Translated by David Ratmoko. Cultural Memory in the Present. Stanford: Stanford University Press, 2009.

———. *The Political Theology of Paul*. Translated by Dana Hollander. Cultural Memory in the Present. Stanford: Stanford University Press, 2004.

Taylor, Charles. *A Secular Age*. Cambridge: Harvard University Press, 2007.

Toscano, Alberto. *Fanaticism: On the Uses of an Idea*. London: Verso, 2010.

Yoder, John Howard. *The Jewish-Christian Schism Revisited*. Edited by Michael G. Cartwright and Peter Ochs. Grand Rapids: Eerdmans, 2003.

———. *Nonviolence: A Brief History*. Edited by Paul Martens, Matthew Porter, and Myles Werntz. Waco, TX: Baylor University Press, 2010.

———. "On Not Being Ashamed of the Gospel: Particularity, Pluralism, and Validation." In *A Pacifist Way of Knowing*, edited by Christian E. Early and Ted Grimsrud, 40–57. Eugene, OR: Cascade, 2010.

———. *The Original Revolution: Essays on Christian Pacifism*. Scottdale, PA: Herald, 2003.

———. *The Politics of Jesus: Vicit Agnus Noster*. Grand Rapids: Eerdmans, 1994.

Yovel, Yirmiyahu. *Spinoza and Other Heretics, Volume 1: The Marrano of Reason*. Princeton, NJ: Princeton University Press, 1992.

Zohar: The Book of Enlightenment. Translated by Daniel Chanan Matt. Ramsey, NJ: Paulist, 1983.

Index